Leader's Guide

DESIGN FOR DISCIPLESHIP

DFD

A NavPress resource published in alliance
with Tyndale House Publishers, Inc.

NAVPRESS●

NavPress is the publishing ministry of The Navigators, an international Christian organization and leader in personal spiritual development. NavPress is committed to helping people grow spiritually and enjoy lives of meaning and hope through personal and group resources that are biblically rooted, culturally relevant, and highly practical.

For more information, visit www.NavPress.com.

DFD Leader's Guide

Copyright © 1973, 1980, 2006 by The Navigators. All rights reserved.

A NavPress resource published in alliance with Tyndale House Publishers, Inc.

NAVPRESS and the NAVPRESS logo are registered trademarks of NavPress, The Navigators, Colorado Springs, CO. TYNDALE is a registered trademark of Tyndale House Publishers, Inc. Absence of ® in connection with marks of NavPress or other parties does not indicate an absence of registration of those marks.

Cover design by Arvid Wallen
Cover illustration by Michael Halbert
Interior design by The DesignWorks Group
Original DFD Author: Chuck Broughton

Revision Team: Dennis Stokes, Judy Gomoll, Christine Weddle, Ralph Ennis

All Scripture quotations, unless otherwise indicated, are taken from the Holy Bible, *New International Version,*® NIV.® Copyright © 1973, 1978, 1984 by Biblica, Inc.® Used by permission. All rights reserved worldwide. Scripture quotations marked *THE MESSAGE* are taken from *THE MESSAGE* by Eugene H. Peterson, copyright © 1993, 1994, 1995, 1996, 2000, 2001, 2002. Used by permission of NavPress Publishing Group. All rights reserved.

ISBN 978-1-60006-011-3

Printed in the United States of America

21 20 19 18 17 16
15 14 13 12 11 10

DFD LG | CONTENTS

Introduction: Getting Started   5

BOOK ONE:
Your Life in Christ   17

BOOK TWO:
The Spirit-Filled Follower of Jesus   39

BOOK THREE:
Walking with Christ   67

BOOK FOUR:
The Character of a Follower of Jesus   89

BOOK FIVE:
Foundations for Faith   111

BOOK SIX:
Growing in Discipleship   133

BOOK SEVEN:
Our Hope in Christ   155

INTRODUCTION: GETTING STARTED

The Bible is a written record of God's love for us. He has given it for our good. From the Scriptures we can begin to know what He is like, what He has done for us, and what He asks us to do — and to be.

But the Navigator Bible study series *Design for Discipleship* is more than a tool for helping someone grow in knowledge of the Scriptures. And your goal as a group leader should be higher than that, too.

Design for Discipleship is a resource for *developing disciples of Jesus Christ.* Knowing more of the Bible is only part of this. Far more important is developing a deep and abiding relationship with God and actually putting into practice what has been learned from the Bible. Don't settle for a lesser aim in your group. Reach high.

Of course the seven *Design for Discipleship* books are only tools. God does the actual work of maturing followers of Jesus. But through a combination of factors — your group's openness to learn, your prayers for them, and your own example of following Jesus — these books can be instruments in the hand of God's Spirit to transform their lives and yours.

WHO SHOULD BE IN THE GROUP?

Design for Discipleship is a comprehensive study of basic biblical principles for following Jesus Christ. It is for everyone who desires to be His disciple. The series can be used by high school students, college students, or adults. It is for married couples and singles, men and women, and families with teenagers.

This series is also appropriate for Sunday school classes and for smaller and less formal groups, such as home Bible studies, "growth" groups, and businessmen's meetings.

Those who are considering a *Design for Discipleship* Bible study should be aware from the beginning that study preparation for each group discussion is necessary — not optional. You may want to show them Book One and page through one of the chapters to let them see how much weekly preparation is involved.

Usually a group size of six to ten is best for discussion. If your group is larger, consider dividing into smaller groups. Also consider asking someone to assist you in leading.

YOUR SCHEDULE

Altogether, the seven *Design for Discipleship* books have thirty-six chapters. A good pace is to study and discuss one chapter per week. However, the goal is growing in Christ — not speeding through each lesson. Your total discussion time each week should probably range from 60-90 minutes. Be sure to start and end on time.

YOUR FIRST MEETING

When your group meets for the first time you will probably find it best to accomplish these three things:

- *Establish a relaxed atmosphere, making sure everyone is acquainted and at ease with you and with each other.*
- *Tell them what they need to know about the* Design for Discipleship *books and about how your group will operate.*

- *Make sure everyone knows what to study in preparation for your next meeting.*

To establish a relaxed atmosphere in a group of people who may not know each other well, spend a few minutes just getting acquainted. Perhaps ask all members to share names, where they grew up, where they live now, what occupations they have, and so on. If you share about yourself first, it will put others more at ease, letting them know how much to say.

Make sure each group member has a Bible and a copy of *Design for Discipleship* Book One. (Bring extra Bibles in case others do not have them.) Explain how they should prepare each chapter. Ask them to commit themselves to prepare each chapter faithfully and attend each discussion for Book One. After that, they can reevaluate their desire to continue in the group.

Have everyone turn to the introduction on page 5 of Book One. Ask various group members to read a paragraph aloud until you have read together the entire introduction. Then ask if they have any questions. You may want to explain in your own words that Book One is about God and His care for us, Jesus Christ and His death and resurrection, and the Holy Spirit's presence in us.

Then turn to page 7 and have someone read the opening paragraphs in chapter 1. To help the group become familiar with the kind of preparation they will be doing on their own each week, answer together some of the questions in this first chapter. You may want to do three or four questions at the beginning, or select a few from other parts of the chapter.

Your aim in this is simply to make them feel at ease about how to complete their study. Have one person read a question aloud, and then have everyone look up the related Scripture reference. Then have someone else read aloud the Scripture passage. You may want to read it from various translations. Talk together about how you would answer the question, and then have each person write the answer in his or her book.

Briefly look over chapter 1 to see how long it is, and tell the group that this is the material they should complete by your next meeting. Confirm the time and place for that meeting.

LEADING THE DISCUSSIONS

As the leader, take charge in a confident way. The group is looking to you for good leadership. But also relax — you don't have to have all the answers!

You may want to experiment with various methods for discussing the study material. One simple approach is to discuss it question by question. You can do this by going around the group in order, with the first person giving his or her answer to question one (followed by discussion), the second person answering question two, and so on.

This method can be a good way to introduce Bible study discussion to those who have never been a part of a Bible study group. The obvious structure gives them a sense of confidence, and they can easily follow the direction of the discussion.

For groups with a bit more experience in Bible study, another discussion method is the section-by-section approach. This can provide more spontaneity. Point out to the group that each chapter in Book One is divided into sections. In chapter 1 these sections are:

- *God Created You*
- *God Is Present and Knows You*
- *God Loves You*
- *God Adopted You into His Family*

LAUNCHING QUESTIONS

Start the discussion by asking the group for its impressions of the first section. Say something like:

"What impressed you most from this section called 'God Created You'?"

> "From this first section, what stood out to you about how God created us?"

This lets members know that you won't be discussing every question in order, but that they are free to share a highlight or observation from *any* question in this section. Of course, starting with a launching question assumes that members have actually completed their own preparation. Remember to direct your question to the entire group rather than to a certain person. These are open-ended questions. That is, they cannot be answered with a "yes" or "no."

FOLLOW-UP QUESTIONS

Someone will probably respond to your open-ended launching question by referring to a specific question in that section. You can invite this person to go a bit deeper by asking:

> "That's interesting, Craig. Would you explain that a bit more?"

> "Would you give us an example of what you mean?"

You can have others share their answers to the same question by asking:

> "What do others think about that question?"

> "Are there any other thoughts on that?"

For example, someone in the group may say that the most impressive thing in the section "God Created You" is what he or she learned from Genesis 1 in question four, that people are created in God's image. A few others may want to comment on this. Then, to discuss the answers more thoroughly, ask one or two thought-provoking follow-up questions that you have prepared beforehand, such as:

"What do you think it means to be created in God's image?"

"What evidence can we see today that every person is created in God's image?"

"How do you think being created in God's image gives us dignity?"

You can then ask others what else most impressed them from this first section. After talking about these and asking questions to stimulate further discussion, go on to the next section. Do not feel obligated to discuss every question. The point of discussing the lesson is for group members to share the more significant thing the Holy Spirit taught them during their time alone.

HEART QUESTIONS

It is important that we engage with the Scriptures at both a head and a heart level. So it is important to ask questions that surface feelings — not just head observations. Proverbs 4:23 indicates that the issues of life come from within the heart. One general way of stating this type of question is to ask:

"What feelings surface within you as you consider this passage [or this section]?"

"How do you feel about [being created in God's image]?"

As a leader, it is important to remember that every person in your group (including you) is still on a journey spiritually. This includes discovering truth cognitively *and* embracing it with the heart. Allow people to be "in process" in their maturing. That is why it is not a good idea to ask, "Do you agree with [someone or something mentioned]?" Forced agreement isn't the point; inviting people to share where they are is more helpful. When you ask, "Does anyone have a different opinion or perspective?" you are inviting them to think for themselves rather than simply conform to what the group thinks.

APPLICATION QUESTIONS

Three important aspects of each lesson are the fundamental ideas of the Scriptures, our heart attitudes, and our intended application from our study. As you lead the discussion be sure to reserve time to discuss your applications. There are already a few application questions embedded in each chapter. Some other ways of asking an application question might be:

"As you consider this chapter, has God impressed something on your heart that He desires for you to apply this week?"

"From everything we've studied in this chapter, do you sense God speaking to you about one particular point to put into practice in your life?"

"What is one thing God might want you to address or change as a result of what you've learned?"

CLOSING THE DISCUSSION

Just as there are several kinds of questions you can ask to lead a good discussion, there are also several ways to bring a discussion to a close. Even if you have not discussed every question from the study, plan to leave the last five to ten minutes of the group time to do one or two of the following closing activities — not all of them.

GOING DEEPER

This is a bonus question provided as an optional way for people to go a bit deeper into the topic. Because it is an optional section, most group members will not have completed it. For others, this section may have been a key part of their study. As you are closing, you might ask a general question such as, "Would anyone like to share what they learned from the Going Deeper section?"

IMAGES AND QUOTES

Each chapter includes one or more quotes, as well as several photos and other images. Sometimes they move us — at other times they might disturb us. Either way, you may want to invite people to comment on any image or quote in the chapter that they connect with.

APPLICATION

Remember to always save time to discuss your personal applications to the Scripture. Otherwise your group may miss an essential part of discipleship. Every chapter already includes one or more questions specifically designed to invite members to apply the truths to their lives. However, if this kind of sharing has not occurred as you reach the end, you might ask a general application question like this: "As you reflect back over your study of Scripture, how have these passages impacted you this week? How do you think God wants you to apply these to your daily life during the coming week?" Occasionally you should share how God has impressed you to apply the study, which will give an example to others in your group about application.

SUMMARY

It is also good at the end of the discussion to provide a brief, broad overview of the chapter, just as it is also good to provide a short review of the previous week's topic at the beginning. Cover the key ideas and how they relate to each other. This can be done in several ways. You might ask a group member to read aloud the various statements listed under the heading "Points to Remember." Or you could ask a general summary question such as, "Let's summarize the chapter. As you consider this chapter as a whole, what one or two truths most stand out to you?"

PRAYER

Plan to spend the last few minutes in prayer. Be aware that some of your group members may not be comfortable yet praying aloud. Invite people to share particular requests briefly, and to pray over their applications from this lesson. Agree with your group members that personal matters shared in the discussion or for prayer should be kept confidential within the group.

SCRIPTURE MEMORY

In Books Two through Seven, members are encouraged to memorize one key verse from the study. This discipline is a valuable way to store God's Word in our hearts. But it is optional. Starting in Book Two, if your group decides to commit to Scripture memory together, you will need to teach them why and how to memorize, as well as keep them motivated. You might encourage members to review their memory verses in pairs as soon as they arrive, or do the review all together at the close of each session. More suggestions for leading others in Scripture memory are provided on pages 41–43 in conjunction with Book Two.

ESTABLISHING A SAFE ENVIRONMENT

A good group discussion involves trust. As people in your group develop trust among them, the quality of your discussions will deepen. As the leader you can guide this process by sharing from your own life in appropriate ways that help promote a safe environment for others to share. That means sharing your struggles and failures, not just your successes and growth. Each time you meet, trust is being developed or eroded. As a leader you can help nurture trust by praying specifically for God to build a safe environment among your group. You may from time to time address this issue by encouraging people to be honest and to keep what is said on a personal basis within the group.

PREPARING FOR EACH DISCUSSION

Two keys to a more interesting and helpful discussion are having an overall objective for each chapter and having good discussion questions prepared ahead of time.

This Leader's Guide includes information that can help you prepare in these two areas. A suggested chapter objective is listed for each chapter in all seven *Design for Discipleship* books. It is both unrealistic and unnecessary for your group to discuss every question in the study guide, because they have already gained from their personal study. So following the chapter objective, we have identified five to ten questions within the study that we think would promote effective discussion. In addition, you will find a few more probing questions that you could select from to go deeper in that section. You will also find space to write your own discussion questions. Many leaders find it helpful to check in their Bible study books the recommended discussion questions, as well as to copy extra questions for discussion in the margins of their books. As you gain more experience leading discussions of the Bible, you will find yourself thinking of effective questions in the midst of the discussion.

At the end of each chapter in this Leader's Guide, you will also find Discussion Tips to help you improve your leadership skills each week. If you have a coleader, you might find it helpful to read these together and coach each other in these skills over time.

Here is a list of the Discussion Tips included throughout this Leader's Guide:

Book 1:1	Listen closely
Book 1:2	Expert leader or facilitator
Book 1:3	Pray, pray, pray
Book 1:4	Refer questions to others
Book 2:1	Helping all to participate
Book 2:2	Helping a talker learn to listen
Book 2:3	End on time
Book 2:4	Start on time

Book 2:5   Sometimes get sidetracked

Book 3:1   Join in prayer together
Book 3:2   Do something together
Book 3:3   Be authentic
Book 3:4   Unanswered questions
Book 3:5   Digging deeper

Book 4:1   Coleading a group
Book 4:2   Listen more closely
Book 4:3   Believe God for change
Book 4:4   Consider starting a new group
Book 4:5   Changing locations

Book 5:1   Intimacy with God
Book 5:2   A grand view of reality
Book 5:3   Issues of the heart
Book 5:4   Loving others
Book 5:5   Care for nature

Book 6:1   Serving outside the group
Book 6:2   Safe sharing environments
Book 6:3   Journal reviews
Book 6:4   Asking for commitment
Book 6:5   Mercy and accountability

May you experience the joy of colaboring with Christ in His kingdom as you lead others and influence them in their spiritual journeys.

BOOK ONE

YOUR LIFE IN CHRIST

1

God Cares for You

CHAPTER OBJECTIVE: To see that we can be assured of our salvation in Christ — an assurance based on scriptural truth.

You can help group members get to know each other better by inviting them to share where they are in their spiritual journeys and what attracted them to participate in this Bible study. Again, you should take the lead in this. Introverted or shy group members may need to be personally asked to share, but not forced.

Remember that your group members have put time and effort into answering the questions in their study book. Many will be eager to share with the group what they have discovered. The focus of your discussion should be on what has impressed them from their own individual study.

You will want to have several discussion questions prepared to help stimulate the group to talk freely about what they have learned. A few suggestions are listed below for each section of chapter 1. Use the space below to write your own discussion questions.

These questions from the chapter may promote the best discussion in your group: 5, 9, 13, 17, and 19. You may want to mark these in your study book somehow to remind you to bring them up if nobody else does.

GOD CREATED YOU (Questions 1–6)

Option 1: You might start the discussion by asking an open-ended "generic" launching question such as, "As you consider this first section, what stood out to you?"

Expect a brief silence while members look over that section. Listen closely to their answers and choose one to ask a follow up question. Remember this pattern can be used for any section of any chapter. The questions we provide here simply supplement this basic discussion-leading approach if you or your group is uncomfortable with this more general, free-flowing approach.

Option 2: You might launch the discussion by asking an open-ended question that relates directly to what people have studied. For instance:

"From this first section, why do you think it is important to realize that God created us?"

"From these first six questions, what difference does it make to you that you are created in the image of God? What does that mean to you as you live this day?"

Be sure to listen closely to their answers. Then, based on their responses, ask follow-up questions. This pattern of asking a launching question, listening closely, and then asking a follow-up question based on their response will help guide a fruitful discussion on any topic.

Suggested for Discussion: Question 5

Use this space to write your own discussion questions for the first section.

GOD IS PRESENT AND KNOWS YOU (Questions 7–9)

Suggested for Discussion: Question 9

David understood that God is present everywhere. How does God's presence impact you?

Do you want to be known by people? Why or why not?

GOD LOVES YOU (Questions 10–14)

Suggested for Discussion: Question 13

Does it make any sense to you that God would love you?

You might ask someone to read aloud the quote from Dallas Willard, following question 11, and comment on it briefly.

GOD ADOPTED YOU INTO HIS FAMILY (Questions 15–19)

Suggested for Discussion: Questions 17 and 19

You may also want someone to read aloud the three assurance verses on pages 17–18.

CLOSING THE DISCUSSION

Select one or more of these activities (not all of them) to close your discussion.

IMAGES AND QUOTES

Invite members to comment on any image or quote in the chapter. It could be one they connected with or one that disturbed them.

SUMMARY

It is often good at the end of the discussion to provide a broad overview of the chapter. Cover the key ideas and how they relate to each other. This can be done by asking a general summary question such as, "Let's summarize the chapter. As you consider this chapter as a whole, what one or two truths stand out to you most?"

Another way to summarize any chapter is to have different group members read aloud the various statements listed under the heading "Points to Remember."

APPLICATION

Remember to discuss your applications to the Scripture. Otherwise your group may miss an essential part of discipleship. You might ask, "As you reflect back over your study of Scripture, how have these passages impacted you this week?" or "How can you apply these to your daily life this coming week?"

GOING DEEPER

Since this is an optional section, some will not have completed it. For others this section may have been a key part of their study. You might want to ask a general question such as, "Would anyone like to share what you learned from the Going Deeper section?"

PRAYER

Plan to spend the last few minutes in prayer. Be aware that some of your group members may not be comfortable praying aloud. Invite people to share particular requests briefly and to pray over their applications from this lesson.

DISCUSSION TIP: LISTEN CLOSELY

Be sure to listen closely to their answers. Then, based on their responses, ask a follow-up question. This pattern of asking a launching question, listening closely, and then asking a follow-up question based on their response will help guide a fruitful discussion.

- Launching question
- Listen carefully
- Follow-up question(s)

2

The Person of Jesus Christ

CHAPTER OBJECTIVE: To see how Jesus Christ is both God and man, and that therefore He is the sole mediator between God and man. Also to be attracted to the Person of Jesus Christ more and more.

Spend the first few minutes of your time together just socializing. If members have not shared about their families, this might be a good way to get to know each other better. As usual, you should set the pace by sharing about your own family briefly.

Begin with a brief summary about what you learned in the last chapter. Then you may want to have someone read aloud the introductory paragraphs at the beginning of this chapter.

> Good questions for discussion are 3, 11, 13, and 15.

THE DEITY OF JESUS CHRIST (Questions 1–11)

You might launch the discussion by asking a general question, such as:

"As you consider this first section, what stood out to you about the deity of Jesus?"

Listen closely to their answers and choose one to ask a follow-up question. Remember this pattern can be used for any section. The questions we provide here simply supplement this approach if you or your group is uncomfortable with this more general, free-flowing approach.

Suggested for Discussion: Questions 3 and 11

How did Jesus demonstrate that He was God?

Since Jesus was born 2,000 years ago, how could He be the Creator?

How is Christ's deity affecting your life today?

THE HUMANITY OF JESUS CHRIST (Questions 12–19)

Suggested for Discussion: Questions 13 and 15

What human characteristics did Jesus exhibit?

Why do you think it was necessary for God to become human and be tempted as we are?

How does Christ's humanity help us relate to God?

As you consider Jesus as both God and man, do you like Him? Why or why not?

There are three quotations in this section. Is there one that particularly touched you?

CLOSING THE DISCUSSION

Select one or more of these activities (not all of them) to close your discussion.

IMAGES AND QUOTES

Invite members to comment on any image or quote in the chapter that they connected with — or that disturbed them.

APPLICATION

Remember to share your applications to the Scripture. Otherwise your group may miss an essential part of discipleship. You might ask, "As you reflect back over your study of Scripture, how have these passages affected you this week?" or "How can you apply these to your daily life this coming week?"

SUMMARY

You might say, "Let's summarize the chapter's main ideas. How do you know Jesus is God? How do you know Jesus is human?" Another way to summarize any chapter is to have different group members read aloud the various statements listed under the heading "Points to Remember."

GOING DEEPER

Since this is an optional section, some will not have completed it. For others this section may have been a key part of their study. You might want to ask a general question such as "Would anyone like to share what you learned from the Going Deeper section?"

PRAYER

Before you pray together to close the meeting, you could have each person share a current prayer request. Reinforce how important it is to keep others' prayer requests confidential.

DISCUSSION TIP: EXPERT LEADER OR FACILITATOR

As the leader, you don't have to have all the answers. You are a discussion facilitator, not an expert Bible theologian. When difficult questions come up in the group, you can admit, "That's an interesting question that I don't have an answer to. Maybe as we go forward we can think about it and return to it later." Or "Would someone like to research that question and respond to it next week?" This shows your group members that, like them, you too are on a spiritual journey and are still growing in your understanding and faith in Christ.

3

The Work of Christ

CHAPTER OBJECTIVE: To gain a better understanding of the elements of the gospel — that Christ died for our sins and was resurrected from the dead for our sake.

Be sure to have clearly in mind the objective for each chapter as you prepare for and lead the chapter discussion. There must be a purpose for your time. It is your responsibility to keep this focus and objective in mind as you lead.

Begin by briefly summarizing the main points of the last chapter — or ask a group member to do this. You could begin the discussion by asking someone to read aloud Edward Clarke's quote on page 50. Also read aloud the opening paragraph in this chapter.

> Good questions for discussion are 5, 8, 10, 16, 17, and 18.

THE LIFE OF JESUS CHRIST (Questions 1–5)

You might launch the discussion by asking a general question:

> "From any of the questions in this first section, what impressed you about the life of Jesus?"

Listen closely to their answers and choose one to ask a follow-up question. Remember this pattern can be used for any section. The questions we provide here simply supplement this approach if you or your group is uncomfortable with this more general, free-flowing approach.

Suggested for Discussion: Question 5
How was Jesus' life different from other men's?

THE DEATH OF JESUS CHRIST (Questions 6–10)

Suggested for Discussion: Questions 8 and 10
What reasons can you give for Jesus' death?

THE RESURRECTION OF JESUS CHRIST (Questions 11–18)

Suggested for Discussion: Questions 16, 17, and 18
Would Jesus' death have any meaning without His resurrection? Explain your answer.

Can a person be a true follower of Jesus and not believe in Christ's resurrection? Why or why not?

Ask someone to read the quote by Philip Yancey, following question 15. What is one thought from this quote that touches you?

CLOSING THE DISCUSSION

Select one or more of these activities (not all of them) to close your discussion.

IMAGES AND QUOTES

Invite members to comment on any image or quote in the chapter that they connected with — or maybe one that disturbed them.

APPLICATION

Remember to share your applications to the Scripture as you go through the study. If necessary at the close you could ask, "As you reflect back over your study of Scripture, how have these passages impacted you this week?" or "How can you apply these to your daily life this coming week?"

SUMMARY

You might ask a group member to read aloud the various statements listed under the heading "Points to Remember." Or you could simply ask, "If God could do it over again, do you think He would permit Jesus to die?"

GOING DEEPER

Since this is an optional section, some will not have completed it. For others this section may have been a key part of their study. You might want to ask a general question such as, "Would anyone like to share what you learned from the Going Deeper section?"

PRAYER

When members share prayer requests, they don't need to explain the whole story behind the request. Urge them (especially by your own example) to explain the request briefly so that your prayer time is spent in prayer — not extended sharing.

DISCUSSION TIP: PRAY, PRAY, PRAY

Leading a Bible discussion is much more about experiencing God than about mastering ideas. Pray that God would draw each person into a deeper intimacy with Him. Also pray for the needs of each person in the group. As you pray for them amazing things will happen!

4

The Spirit Within You

CHAPTER OBJECTIVE: To understand that the Holy Spirit lives in all who believe in Christ, and enables us to obey Christ.

By now your group members should be well acquainted with one another, but they will still want a few minutes to catch up or talk about how the week has gone. If you show that you recognize the worth of every person in the group, the others will follow your example and will also respect and appreciate each other.

As usual, you might begin by referring briefly to what you studied in the previous chapter. You might launch the discussion by asking someone to read aloud the opening paragraph, or by discussing the quote by A. W. Tozer after question 8.

At the end of this session, point out to the group that the Wheel Illustration on page 74 in their study book serves as the outline for their study in Book Two. The five chapters in Book Two cover the five topics of obedience, God's Word, prayer, fellowship, and witnessing. You may want to have the group learn this illustration and be able to draw and explain it to someone else.

Good questions for discussion are 3, 4, 6, 11, 12, and 20.

THE COMING OF THE HOLY SPIRIT (Questions 1–3)

You might launch the discussion by asking a general question such as:

> "As you consider this first section, what stood out to you about the coming of the Holy Spirit?"

Listen closely to their answers and choose one to ask a follow-up question. Remember this pattern can be used for any section. The questions we provide here simply supplement this approach if you or your group is uncomfortable with this more general, free-flowing approach.

Suggested for Discussion: Question 3

Why do you think God sent the Holy Spirit after Jesus?

What difference would that make to you if God had not sent the Holy Spirit?

JESUS' WORK TODAY (Questions 4–8)

Suggested for Discussion: Questions 4 and 6

What is Jesus doing today?

As you live your daily life, what impact do Jesus' current actions have on you?

THE INDWELLING OF THE HOLY SPIRIT (Questions 9–11)

Suggested for Discussion: Question 11

How can a person know that he or she has the Holy Spirit?

THE LEADING OF THE HOLY SPIRIT (Questions 12–18)

Suggested for Discussion: Question 12

How have you sensed the Holy Spirit leading you in a specific way?

How have you experienced the Holy Spirit helping you in a specific way?

THE FILLING OF THE HOLY SPIRIT (Questions 19–20)

Suggested for Discussion: Question 20

What seems to be the relationship between being controlled by the Holy Spirit, being indwelt by the Holy Spirit, and being filled by the Holy Spirit?

How do you feel about being controlled, indwelt, and filled? What emotions surface as you consider these realities?

What is the Holy Spirit doing today in your life?

Discuss the Wheel Illustration with your group. You may want to use a large flip chart and actually draw this illustration, explaining each part as you draw. Perhaps challenge them to study this helpful diagram until they can explain it to someone else simply and clearly.

CLOSING THE DISCUSSION

Select one or more of these activities (not all of them) to close your discussion.

IMAGES AND QUOTES

Invite members to comment on any image or quote in the chapter that they connected with — or maybe one that disturbed them.

APPLICATION

Remember to discuss your applications to the Scripture. You might ask, "As you reflect back over your study of Scripture, how have these passages impacted you this week?" or "How can you apply these to your daily life this coming week?"

SUMMARY

Ask a group member to read aloud the various statements listed under the heading "Points to Remember." Or ask group members to complete this sentence: "From this study, I know the Holy Spirit lives within me because . . ."

GOING DEEPER

Since this is an optional section, some will not have completed it. For others this section may have been a key part of their study. You might want to ask a general question such as "Would anyone like to share what you learned from the Going Deeper section?"

REVIEW

Since this is the last chapter in Book One, devote a few minutes to reviewing your time together over the last weeks. Encourage members to continue studying Book Two. You might ask review questions such as:

How did you like Book One?

What was the most helpful thing from our study together over these weeks?

Would you like to go into Book Two?

Is there anything we need to change in order to enrich our time together?

Then hand out Book Two to those who will continue, and agree on the next assignment and meeting arrangements.

As members share their requests, write them down in a small notebook. This communicates that you truly want to remember and pray over each request mentioned. Ask members to share how God has already answered requests they mentioned in the previous weeks together. Spend time praising God for His goodness and faithfulness to us.

DISCUSSION TIP: REFER QUESTIONS TO OTHERS

Sometimes group members will want to make you the expert. If they tend to direct their questions to you as the leader, you can sometimes refer these questions to others by asking, "That's a great question. What do the rest of you think about it?"

ASSESSING YOUR LEADERSHIP

You can use these self-assessment questions following each session to help you improve your leadership in the future. If you have a coleader, discuss these questions together after each discussion and make adjustments where you see room for improvement.

1. Did you know the material well enough to have freedom in leading?
2. Did you have enough questions prepared to properly guide the discussion?
3. Did you listen closely to others' answers in order to ask good follow-up questions?
4. Did you discuss the major points in the chapter?
5. Are people growing in trusting each other? Are they sharing their hearts as well as their minds?
6. Was the discussion practical?
7. Did everyone participate?
8. Did you begin and end on time?

THE SPIRIT-FILLED
FOLLOWER OF JESUS

Book Two
Introduction

Beginning in Book Two, your group will be encouraged to commit one verse from each chapter to memory. If your group members are not experienced in memorizing Scripture, the following material will help you motivate them to begin this spiritual discipline. Consider sharing just one or two of the following verses each week as your members review their verses together.

WHY MEMORIZE SCRIPTURE?

You won't find the word "memorize" in the Bible. Instead we are encouraged to hide it in our hearts, meditate on it, and never neglect it (Psalm 119:9-16).

- *"Bind [my commands] around your neck, write them on the tablet of your heart." (Proverbs 3:3)*
- *"Keep my words and store up my commands within you. Keep my commands and you will live; guard my teachings as the apple of your eye. Bind them on your fingers; write them on the tablet of your heart." (Proverbs 7:1-3)*

- *"It is pleasing when you keep them in your heart." (Proverbs 22:18)*
- *"Meditate on [God's words] day and night." (Joshua 1:8)*

These verses and others also explain the reasons for and benefits of memorizing Scripture:

- *"That I might not sin against you . . . [my] feet do not slip."*
  (Psalm 119:11; 37:31)
- *"They are life to those who find them and health to one's whole body."*
  (Proverbs 4:22)
- *"You will win favor and a good name in the sight of God and man."*
  (Proverbs 3:4)
- *"Your trust may be in the LORD." (Proverbs 22:19)*
- *"You may be careful to do everything written in it. Then you will be*
  prosperous and successful." (Joshua 1:8)
- So that you will *"have all of them ready on your lips." (Proverbs 22:18)*
- *"Your words . . . [are] my joy and my heart's delight." (Jeremiah 15:16)*

Perhaps even more compelling than these reasons is seeing how powerfully God can use a person who has taken the time and effort to consistently memorize Scripture. When Jesus faced Satan (Matthew 4:4-11), He drew from the many verses of Scripture that He had memorized in His youth to pinpoint Satan's deception and resist temptation. When Peter addressed the huge crowd on the day of Pentecost, he was given no time to consult his concordance and prepare a message! Because he had made Scripture memory a priority in his life, he could quote from three different Old Testament passages that helped bring 3,000 people to the Lord!

❝ I am amazed at the countless times God has pulled from my mind a memorized verse that has been exactly the right thing at the right time! At times it was comfort. At other time He gave guidance, a push ahead or a pull to stop, a reminder of His promise, a prompting for wisdom, a word for counseling another, or an insight for those seeking our Lord. ❞

—Dennis Stokes, Navigator Staff

If you long to equip yourself to counteract Satan, resist sin, trust and obey God, listen to God's voice, and minister to others, there is no better investment of your time than memorizing Scripture.

A good place to begin is by considering what the Bible says about the value and benefits of storing up God's Word in our hearts through memorization. Then you will need to show the group how to memorize a verse. (See the *Topical Memory System* or *TMS* by The Navigators for practical help in this.) You should explore several creative ways to build memory review into their daily routines.

Encourage members to copy each verse onto a small card, and to carry their verse cards with them. Other review tips include: Put your memory verses on your computer's screen saver. Review them out loud — *often!* Write them out until you can write them accurately. Meditate on them. Pray over them. Tell a friend what they mean to you. Put yourself to sleep at night thinking about them. And look forward to listening to God speak to you! The key to remembering verses over time is to review . . . review . . . and review some more!

Excerpted from "The Heartbeat of Jesus" Bible study. ©2005. Used by permission of The Navigators' National Training Team

As you begin studying Book Two, it is worth your time to go back to the first few pages of this Leader's Guide to refresh your memory of leading and guiding principles. Consider specifically how you would like to develop as a Bible study leader during your study of Book Two. Ask God to help you mature as a man or woman of the Word.

1

The Obedient Follower of Jesus

CHAPTER OBJECTIVE: To see that obedience based on trust is the most important quality of our love for Jesus Christ.

You may want to begin this session by reading the introduction to Book Two starting on page 5. Then review the Wheel Illustration on page 7 — a tool for helping us assess how balanced we are in our walks with Christ. Encourage members to learn how to draw this illustration while explaining the elements to someone else.

At the beginning of this session, it is important to discuss the benefits of memorizing Scripture with your group. You might read through the overview of Scripture memory principles provided in this Leader's Guide. Also share your own convictions and practice of memorizing Scripture verses. Let your group decide if they will commit to memorizing one verse per week for the duration of Book Two. If they agree, devote time at the end of this session to helping them memorize together the verse for this week.

Good questions for discussion are 4, 8, 11, 15, 16, 19, and 20.

A BASIS FOR OBEDIENCE: BEHOLDING GOD (Questions 1–7)

You might launch the discussion by asking a general question such as, "As you consider this first section, what stood out to you?"

Listen closely to their answers and choose one to ask a follow-up question. Remember this pattern can be used for any section. The questions we provide here simply supplement this approach if you or your group is uncomfortable with this more general, free-flowing approach.

Suggested for Discussion: Question 4

How does our understanding of who God is influence our obedience to Him?

Why is it for our good to obey God?

How important is love in our relationship with God?

OBEYING GOD'S DESIRES FOR YOUR LIFE (Questions 8–12)

Suggested for Discussion: Questions 8 and 11
Why is the Bible crucial in the matter of obedience?

LIVING OBEDIENTLY (Questions 13–20)

Suggested for Discussion: Questions 15, 16, 19, and 20
Describe God's part and your part in your living an obedient life.

Why are our attitudes important in obedience?

What is the difference between temptation and sin?

Do people fall into sin or plan for it?

What is God's remedy for sin?

Even though God knows everything, why should we confess our sins?

In what areas of your life have you had victory over sin lately?

CLOSING THE DISCUSSION

As you bring the discussion to a close, remember to leave the last five or ten minutes to share one or more of the following activities. You might ask anyone who completed the Going Deeper section to share a highlight. Or include time to share personal applications from the study, or for someone to summarize the lesson.

PRAYER

Remember to pray faithfully and regularly for your group members. Each one will have distinct needs you can pray about. Learn what these are. Encourage group members to use their prayer lists each week, and to pray for each other throughout the week.

SUGGESTED SCRIPTURE MEMORY

Discuss with your group the value of memorizing Scripture. Ask them what benefits they see in memorizing the Word of God. Ask them if they would like to review verses each week. If so, you may begin this week or next. There are many creative ways to review memory verses together: reciting aloud together, reciting individually with a partner, or writing out the verse. Vary how you review verses each week. Today, take time to help members actually memorize the verse together, using topic and reference first, and adding one phrase at a time. Aim for word perfect memorizing — not paraphrasing. Repeat several times out loud until members are confident.

DISCUSSION TIP: HELPING ALL TO PARTICIPATE

As a facilitator, one of your goals is to involve everyone in the discussion. Some people have difficulty speaking up in a group. Without putting them on the spot too often, you might want to direct a question to those individuals occasionally.

2

God's Word in Your Life

CHAPTER OBJECTIVE: To become convinced of the importance of the Scriptures as God's personal communication to us; to decide to spend time each day in reading the Scriptures.

You could have the group review their verses from the last chapter and this chapter at the beginning of each discussion session, perhaps while they wait for other group members to arrive. Or you could do this at the close of the session. Tell them how important Scripture memory is to you. Set the pace by quoting the verse yourself for your group.

Be sure to discuss — and better yet, demonstrate — the Hand Illustration on page 42.

> Good discussion questions are 4, 8, 12, 13, and 16.

GOD'S WORD — HIS COMMUNICATION TO YOU (Questions 1–6)

You might launch the discussion by asking a general question such as, "From these first six questions about God's Word, what stood out to you about God's communication with us?"

Suggested for Discussion: Question 4

How do you know the Bible is God's Word?

How does the Bible spiritually refresh you?

How does the Bible reflect God's character?

Is God's truth absolute or relative? Why? And what difference does it make?

HOW THE BIBLE HELPS YOU (Questions 7–8)

Suggested for Discussion: Question 8

How is the Bible like bread (Matthew 4:4)?

How is the Bible like a mirror (James 1:23-25)?

How is the Bible like fire and a hammer (Jeremiah 23:29)?

How has the Bible helped you recently?

BECOMING A MAN OR WOMAN OF THE WORD (Questions 9–13)

Suggested for Discussion: Questions 12 and 13

Why does God hold us responsible for knowing the Scriptures?

What does it mean to let the Word of Christ dwell richly in us?

THE IMPORTANCE OF MEDITATION (Questions 14–16)

Suggested for Discussion: Question 16

What is meditation?

How can we meditate on Scripture day and night?

How is a person's stability based on his or her relationship with God through the Scriptures?

How do you think your heart can respond to the living Word of God?

CLOSING THE DISCUSSION

In closing this week's discussion, you may ask members to comment on Images and Quotes, to share personal Applications, or to share from the Going Deeper section. Take time to demonstrate the Hand Illustration — not in drawing it but by using your own hand and Bible. Be sure to explain the benefits of and the differences between each of the five methods for taking in God's Word. Encourage each member to share this illustration with a friend during the week.

PRAYER

Close your time together in prayer. Remember to spend more time actually praying than you do sharing prayer requests. God already knows the details behind each request. Also encourage people to share how God has answered requests they mentioned in previous weeks. Include praise in your prayer time.

SCRIPTURE MEMORY REVIEW

If your group has agreed to memorize and review Scripture together, be sure to reserve time for review. Review the verse for this chapter and also the verse from the last chapter.

DISCUSSION TIP: HELPING A TALKER LEARN TO LISTEN

Discussions are dialogues between people. If some people in your group have difficulty listening, you might want to talk to them outside the context of the discussion. Tell them that you have noticed others are speaking up less than they are. Ask them if they can help create a healthy dialogue among the whole group by speaking less and listening more. Ask if listening comes easy for them. They may process information better as they speak. Help them see that they need to give space for others to speak, just as they need space to learn to listen.

3

Conversing with God

CHAPTER OBJECTIVE: To see prayer as our God-given means of communication with Him, and to decide to spend time each day in prayer.

At the end of the session, encourage your group members to begin using a prayer list.

Motivation is a key factor in learning. Help your group members see why learning the biblical view of discipleship is important.

> Good questions for discussion are 1, 3, 6, 7, 11, 13, 16, 18, and 19.

PRAYER — YOUR TWO-WAY COMMUNICATION WITH GOD

(Questions 1–6)

You might launch the discussion by asking a general question such as,

"In this first section on prayer, what impressed you most about communicating with God?"

Suggested for Discussion: Questions 1, 3, and 6

What is necessary on our part to develop a relationship with God?

What does it mean to "pray continually" (1 Thessalonians 5:17)?

What attitudes or emotions do you have in coming to God in prayer?

THE BENEFITS OF PRAYER (Questions 7–11)

Suggested for Discussion: Questions 7 and 11

If you could spend an hour with God and say anything at all, what would you say? What would you ask Him?

What will be the results in our lives of meeting with God in prayer?

CONDITIONS OF PRAYER (Questions 12–14)

Suggested for Discussion: Question 13

Why is faith (or trust) essential when praying (Matthew 21:22)?

What does it mean to ask in Jesus' name (John 16:24)?

Should you pray if your heart really isn't in it? Why, or why not?

FOR WHOM DO YOU PRAY? (Questions 15–21)

Suggested for Discussion: Questions 16, 18, and 19

What did you learn about prayer from Paul's prayer in Ephesians 3:14-21?

Are there people in your life who have mistreated you? Spend some time now talking with God about them and your response to them.

Have you found it helpful to use a prayer list? If so, how?

As the leader, pause to explain how you have used a prayer list in the past; show group members a page from your own prayer list. Pass out a blank prayer list to each member, and suggest that they use it to record requests shared in your group.

CLOSING THE DISCUSSION

Select one or more of the following ways to close your discussion: Going Deeper, Application, Images and Quotes, or ask a Summary question such as, "Are you consistently meeting with God daily for time alone in prayer and Scripture reading and meditation? Tell us about that time."

PRAYER

Invite members to share how they experienced the prayer pause on page 67. Then use the prayer list to record each others' requests before praying together.

SCRIPTURE MEMORY REVIEW

If your group has agreed to memorize and review Scripture together, be sure to reserve time for review. Review the verse for this week and previous weeks. Ask someone to share how a memorized verse helped him or her throughout the week.

DISCUSSION TIP: END ON TIME

The dread of any discussion group is a leader who cannot keep track of time! Pace yourself. End on time, even if people don't come on time. If the discussion is going great, you might say, "Our time is over, so let's close. If anyone wants to keep on discussing, we can continue after those who need to leave have an opportunity to do so." By sticking to your time frame, your group members will appreciate you for respecting their time.

4

Fellowship with Followers of Jesus

CHAPTER OBJECTIVE: To see that fellowship with other followers of Jesus is a biblical command, based on our need for each other.

In planning the discussion, it is often best to develop questions for the main study material first, and then plan how you will begin and end the discussion.

> Good questions for discussion are 1, 8, 12, 14, 15, 17, and 19.

WHAT IS BIBLICAL FELLOWSHIP? (Questions 1–6)

You might launch the discussion by asking a general question, such as, "From this first section, what conclusions did you come to about biblical fellowship?"

Suggested for Discussion: Question 1
  When does fellowship take place?

  What are the most important things we can share with others?

  Are you satisfied with the level of fellowship you have with others?

THE PURPOSE OF FELLOWSHIP (Questions 7–10)

Suggested for Discussion: Question 8
  How do we stimulate each other to love and to do good works?

  Explain why fellowship is important to you. How have you benefited from relating to other followers of Jesus?

THE BODY OF CHRIST (Questions 12–15)

Suggested for Discussion: Questions 12, 14, and 15
  When it comes to fellowship, how can Christ be first in our lives?

  Why are all members necessary in the body of Christ?

  Are you satisfied with the part you are playing in the body of Christ? Explain.

  Do you ever struggle with feeling superior or inferior to others in the body of Christ whose functions are different from yours? If so, how do you deal with these feelings?

THE LOCAL CHURCH (Questions 16–20)

Suggested for Discussion: Questions 17 and 19
  What particular "works of service" (Ephesians 4:12) are you active in right now that God is using to build up others in the body of Christ?

  What does God want you to do with regard to prayer and financial support for your spiritual leaders?

CLOSING THE DISCUSSION

Select one or more of the following ways to close your discussion: Going Deeper, Application, Images and Quotes, or a Summary.

PRAYER

This is a good time to share answers to prayer requests and issues that members have shared before. Praise God for His faithfulness and continue to pray for ongoing needs. Encourage members to write requests on their prayer lists.

Also look briefly at the next chapter. Explain that it will require extra time to prepare because they will be asked to write out their own story of trusting Christ. Satan will oppose this activity, so be praying for each other to reflect on and express their stories in fresh ways.

SCRIPTURE MEMORY REVIEW

If your group has agreed to memorize and review Scripture together, be sure to reserve time for review. Review the memory verse for this chapter together several times. Since there is only one chapter left in Book Two, consider devoting a few extra minutes to Scripture memory review. Consider passing out paper to each person and asking them write out from memory the four verses from chapters 1–4. Then exchange papers to have others check for accuracy.

DISCUSSION TIP: START ON TIME

Sometimes people will begin to drift in late rather than come on time. One option is to renegotiate the starting time. Another option is to begin on time even if everyone isn't present yet. By starting on time, people will generally adjust by showing up on time.

5

Witnessing

CHAPTER OBJECTIVE: To see the importance of sharing with others what Jesus Christ has done for us, and to become more skilled in doing this.

Begin your discussion by reading the introduction to this chapter. Discuss briefly what witnessing for Jesus has in common with matchmaking.

Allow plenty of time in this session for each group member to read aloud his or her personal testimony. Find something to affirm in each testimony, and perhaps mention one way in which it could be improved. Remember that these stories are very significant and personal. Also remember that discussion involves personal feelings as well as objective opinions about the subject matter. Don't make the mistake of being insensitive to these personal feelings.

You might suggest *The Insider* by Jim Petersen and Mike Shamy as outside reading on this topic.

> Good questions for discussion are 2, 7, 8, 11, 12, 16, 17, and 19.

THE OPPORTUNITY (Questions 1–7)

Perhaps launch the discussion by asking a general question such as, "As you consider this first section, what stood out to you about our opportunities to share Christ with others?

Suggested for Discussion: Questions 2 and 7
Why was Peter compelled to speak of Jesus?

How should seeking God's approval be a motive in our witnessing?

Our attitudes can make all the difference in witnessing. What are some less than desirable attitudes you have observed? And what are some desirable attitudes you have observed in believers sharing their faith?

HOW DO YOU EFFECTIVELY WITNESS? (Questions 8–16)

Suggested for Discussion: Questions 8, 11, 12, and 16
Why is love so important in witnessing?

What qualities make a person an effective witness?

How much do you need to know in order to speak to someone about your faith in Christ?

What might hinder you from sharing your faith in Jesus with others?

PAUL'S STORY (Questions 17–18)

Suggested for Discussion: Question 17

What kind of man was Paul before he met Christ?

How did Christ change Paul?

What can you learn from Paul's story that is helpful to you?

YOUR STORY (Question 19)

Suggested for Discussion After Sharing Our Stories: Question 19

Why is it important to write out your story of how you became a follower of Jesus?

As the leader, be sure to reserve ample time for people to read the story of how they trusted Christ. After each person shares, respond with an encouraging comment about the impact of his or her story on you personally, or how you think it may impact others who are considering trusting in Christ. Don't be critical; rather, be affirming. If there isn't enough time for all to share, be sure to plan time at your next meeting for the rest to read their stories.

CLOSING THE DISCUSSION

Select one or more of the following ways to close your discussion: Going Deeper, Application, Images and Quotes, or a Summary.

PRAYER

Take time to pray for one another and to praise God for all He is doing in your lives.

SCRIPTURE MEMORY REVIEW

Close by quoting the memory verse for this chapter together as a group, as well as in pairs to check for accuracy. Encourage members to review these five verses daily, as well as the verses from Book One.

REVIEW

This is the last chapter in Book Two. Perhaps it is time to review what has helped you most in your spiritual journey from everything you have studied in Book Two. Also discuss your plans to move on to Book Three. Ask members if there is anything you need to change to enrich your time together. Pass out copies of Book Three to those who will be continuing.

DISCUSSION TIP: SOMETIMES GET SIDETRACKED

Sometimes people may want to discuss an idea that is slightly off the topic of the chapter. That's okay. It may seem irrelevant to you, but it is probably quite relevant to them. Your willingness to discuss their questions and ideas will help build trust. Then you can redirect the discussion back to the main ideas of the lesson.

HOW TO PRAY FOR YOUR GROUP

Your most important preparation for each session is prayer. You will want to make your requests personal, but here are some suggestions for praying each week:

Pray that everyone in the group will complete the chapter preparation and attend this week's discussion. Ask God to help each of them to share their thoughts honestly and to make a significant contribution to the discussion.

Ask God to give each of them an understanding of what they study. Pray that God will meet the unique needs of each person through this exposure to His Word. Pray for the specific requests people share within the group.

Pray that, as the leader, you will know the Holy Spirit's guidance in exercising patience, acceptance, sensitivity, and wisdom. Pray for an atmosphere of genuine love in the group, with each member being honestly open to learning and changing. Do all you can to build an environment of grace and nonjudgmentalism.

Pray that the result of your study and discussion will be that each person grows more deeply in love with Jesus and has greater confidence in the Bible and a willingness to obey the Lord by applying the Scriptures you study.

WALKING WITH CHRIST

1

Maturing in Christ

CHAPTER OBJECTIVE: To recognize that spiritual growth is a lifelong process during which God transforms us increasingly into the image of Christ as we yield to Him — a process that includes victories and defeats, struggles and successes, as well as tests to our character.

Encourage your group in Scripture memory, and allow time for reviewing verses they learned in Books One and Two. Decide whether members should review their verses at the beginning of your time together or at the end. Each week, select a creative way to review verses so that you do not get in a rut.

Perhaps plan for a social or recreational activity with your group outside your discussion sessions.

Have someone read aloud the introduction to Book Three on page 5.

> Good questions for discussion include 1, 5, 12, 15, and 18.

YOUR STARTING POINT (Questions 1–4)

You might launch the discussion by asking a general question such as, "As you consider this first section, what was the starting point in your journey with Christ?"

Always listen closely to their answers and choose one to ask a follow-up question. Remember this pattern can be used for any section. The questions we provide here simply supplement this approach if you or your group is uncomfortable with this more general, free-flowing approach.

Suggested for Discussion: Question 1

What has God provided to help you mature spiritually?

Are you more mature today than you were a year ago? How do you know?

MOVING TOWARD MATURITY (Questions 5–9)

Suggested for Discussion: Question 5

What is "unity in the faith" (Ephesians 4:13)?

What characterizes a spiritually mature person?

THE PROCESS OF GROWTH (Questions 10–13)

Suggested for Discussion: Question 12

How can you measure physical maturity? How can you measure spiritual maturity?

What do you think it would look like for a follower of Christ to "reign in life" (Romans 5:17)?

Specifically what would it look like for you to "reign in life" at this point in your spiritual journey?

HOW TO LIVE (Question 14) AND THE MATURE LIFE
(Questions 15–19)

Suggested for Discussion: Questions 15 and 18

In what ways do you encounter good and evil in your daily life?

When you face evil, do you usually desire that justice or mercy will triumph? (See James 2:12-13.)

What are some areas in which you have experienced spiritual growth?

CLOSING THE DISCUSSION

Be sure to leave five to ten minutes of your time together to bring the discussion to a close. There are several ways you might do this. You might ask a group member to summarize what you have discussed, either by reading the Points to Remember, stating the key things the group has concluded, or by asking a general summary question such as, "What do you think are the primary areas in which you are now growing spiritually?"

Another way to close the discussion is to invite anyone who completed the optional section (Going Deeper) to share a highlight. Every chapter already includes a few questions that invite members to share personal applications. However, you might close by asking a few to share how they will respond to the study and apply something from it in their lives.

You could also invite members to select one image — or one quotation — from the chapter and comment on its impact in their lives. As the leader, you should plan which of these closing activities is best for your group before you end in prayer.

PRAYER

If your group has been meeting together for some time — say, through Books One and Two — people should be growing more comfortable in sharing prayer requests and in praying out loud together. As you close this session in prayer, remind members that maturing spiritually is a mysterious process that we can hinder, but only God can complete. Praise Him for each step of growth you see in one another. Also consider the prayer suggestions in the Discussion Tip below.

SCRIPTURE MEMORY REVIEW

If your group has agreed to memorize and review Scripture together, be sure to reserve time for review. Since this is the beginning of a new book, perhaps take the time to review the suggestions for Scripture memory found on pages 43–45. Be creative in motivating members to memorize, and occasionally vary the method you use to review verses together.

DISCUSSION TIP: JOIN IN PRAYER TOGETHER

Each person in your group has special needs on his or her heart. Maybe he or she is concerned for a test, health issues, money problems, or relationships. We all have needs. And we can bring these needs before God together. Consider praying for each other during the week between discussions. One option is to form prayer partners.

2

The Lordship of Christ

CHAPTER OBJECTIVE: To see that trusting Christ to control our lives is the only way to have a fulfilling life, and to learn how to give Him that control.

Encourage your group to set personal goals in each area of the Wheel and Hand Illustrations. Provide a pattern for them by developing and sharing with them your own goals. For example, in the area of prayer from the Wheel Illustration, your goal could be to pray through several issues on your prayer list every day. In the area of reading (from the Hand Illustration), your goal could be to read through the whole Bible in the next twelve months by reading three or four chapters each day.

Encourage your group members to review their Scripture memory verses in pairs while they wait for the rest of the members to arrive.

> Good questions for discussion include 2, 7, 9, 13, 14, 17, and 20.

THE LORD JESUS CHRIST (Questions 1–6)

Your lead-off question to begin the discussion on each section should be a "how" or "why" question, and should be directed to the group as a whole rather than to a particular person.

You might launch the discussion of this first section by asking a general question such as, "Before we talk about the Lordship of Jesus, why do you think Jesus is called 'Lord' in the Bible?" or "As you consider this first section, did anything stand out to you?"

Suggested for Discussion: Question 2

What does the word "lord" mean to you in describing a person? (Consider "landlord" and "warlord" and "lording it over" someone.)

What are some of the ways Jesus is Lord?

How do you feel about Jesus being "the Lord"?

ACKNOWLEDGE HIS LORDSHIP BY DECISION (Questions 7–12)

Suggested for Discussion: Questions 7 and 9

What right does Christ have to be Lord over your life?

What is involved in surrendering to Christ's lordship?

What are the alternatives to making Christ the Lord of your life?

Do you feel that most followers of Jesus actively submit to Christ's lordship? Why or why not?

What have you done to show your response to Christ's lordship?

ACKNOWLEDGE HIS LORDSHIP IN PRACTICE (Question 13)
AND REALITY CHECK (Questions 14–20)

Suggested for Discussion: Questions 13, 14, 17, and 20

What does it mean to humble ourselves "under God's mighty hand" (1 Peter 5:6)?

What is the connection between being humble and casting all our cares on God?

When do you keep cares and worries to yourself?

What is a good way to evaluate if Jesus is truly Lord of your life?

What does the lordship of Christ mean to you personally?

CLOSING THE DISCUSSION

This topic really lends itself to personal application. Whatever else you do to summarize and close the session, be sure to allow time for members to share applications. Consider a general question such as, "In what areas have you experienced growth in submitting to Christ's lordship?"

PRAYER

In prayer, focus on Christ as the Lord of all *and* as the Lord of your life and maturing process.

SCRIPTURE MEMORY REVIEW

Are your group members using verse cards for memorizing and reviewing Scripture memory verses? If not, take the time to reinforce the value of using verse cards. Also provide several blank cards for them to use during their study in Book Three.

DISCUSSION TIP: DO SOMETHING TOGETHER

Trusting relationships are formed through dialogue and also by doing things together. Consider serving others together, going to dinner together, watching a good movie together, going camping, and so on. As your group moves into action, the depth of dialogue will usually deepen.

CHAPTER

3

Faith and the Promises of God

CHAPTER OBJECTIVE: To know that our faith should be based on the promises of God in the Bible, and that, no matter how long it takes, we can trust God to fulfill His promises to us and can stake our lives on His faithfulness.

> Good questions for discussion include 1, 4, 5, 9, 10, 11, 13, and 17.

WALKING BY FAITH (Questions 1–6)

Help each group member realize that it is his or her responsibility both to contribute to and profit from the group discussion. You might launch the discussion by asking a general question such as, "As you consider this first section, how does the Bible describe faith?"

Suggested for Discussion: Questions 1, 4, and 5

How are faith and trust similar?

Why is faith so important in following Jesus?

How can we face our doubts honestly while growing in faith?

If you are facing a difficult circumstance now, how can you respond to it by trusting in God's faithfulness?

OBJECTS OF FAITH (Questions 7–9)

Suggested for Discussion: Question 9

Which is more important — the amount of faith we have or the object of our faith? Why?

Is faith something we receive from God or something we place in God? Explain.

EXAMPLES OF FAITH (Question 10)

Suggested for Discussion: Question 10

How can we follow the examples of faith in Hebrews 11?

THE PROMISES OF GOD (Questions 11–13)

Suggested for Discussion: Questions 11 and 13

What is a promise?

How have promises kept — or promises broken — impacted you?

PROMISES TO CLAIM (Questions 14–19)

Suggested for Discussion: Question 17

What does it mean to claim a promise?

Why did God make promises to His children?

What is one scriptural promise you can claim now?

CLOSING THE DISCUSSION

As you close the discussion during this session, consider asking a summary question such as, "What promises from God are you claiming for your life?" Or consider doing together the Going Deeper section, which explores some wonderful things about God that invite us to trust Him in faith.

Also encourage the group to allow plenty of time before your next session for thinking through and completing the chart preceding question 19 in chapter 4.

PRAYER

If you used the Going Deeper section to close your discussion, also consider using the list of God's attributes to lead you into a time of worship and praise to God.

SCRIPTURE MEMORY REVIEW

As you review your memory verses, notice which members may have dropped behind and become discouraged. Make it a point to spend one-on-one time with these people during the coming week to strengthen in Scripture memory — or any other way.

DISCUSSION TIP: BE AUTHENTIC

An authentic leader is always more helpful in our spiritual journeys than a leader who has all the answers and no difficulties. You might not need to share the complete depths of your struggles with everyone, but be real . . . be authentic. Your group can be a great support to you as you share your real life with them. As you are vulnerable and trust your group members with the real you, you will also be creating an environment of grace where they will feel safe enough to be authentic, too.

4

Knowing God's Will

CHAPTER OBJECTIVE: To learn how to practically seek and know God's will.

Since there is only one more chapter in Book Three, now would be a good time to devote a few extra minutes to reviewing your verses from this book — including this week's verse.

> Good questions for discussion include 2, 5, 6, 7, and 13. And in Principles in Practice: What is the main thing you learned? *What is the most important principle in decision making to you?*

THE REVEALED WILL OF GOD (Questions 1–5)

You might launch the discussion by asking someone to read the introduction to this chapter. Invite people to respond to Paul Little's description of the will of God, if they can relate to it. Then launch into the first section by asking a general question such as, "From these first few questions, what impressed you most about God's revealed will?"

Suggested for Discussion: Questions 2 and 5

How far in advance can we expect God to reveal His will to us?

Why is it essential for us to understand God's will?

What are specific things God wants for every follower of Jesus?

PRINCIPLES OF DECISION MAKING (Questions 6–18)

Suggested for Discussion: Questions 6, 7, and 13

As you review the many methods to determine God's will, which have you tried?

How would you explain Matthew 6:33 to a younger follower of Jesus?

What is your understanding of a holy life (1 Peter 1:15)?

What does it mean to be conformed to this world?

How does the Holy Spirit guide us?

What qualities would you look for in someone you go to for counsel?

Consider James 1:5. Do you ask God for wisdom? Is He answering? Explain.

How can we know our decisions are based on God's will?

PRINCIPLES IN PRACTICE (Questions 19–27)

Suggested for Discussion:

What is the main thing you learned in filling out this chart?

What is the most important principle in decision making to you?

CLOSING THE DISCUSSION

In closing this week's discussion, you may ask members to comment on Images and Quotes or to share personal Applications. In addition, consider summarizing the lesson by demonstrating the God's Will Hand Illustration in the Going Deeper section.

PRAYER

Is any member of your group seeking God's will on a specific decision? If so, come alongside that person and pray with him or her.

SCRIPTURE MEMORY REVIEW

If your group has agreed to memorize and review Scripture together, be sure to reserve time for review. Review the verse for this week and previous weeks. Ask people how Scripture memory is helping them throughout the week.

DISCUSSION TIP: UNANSWERED QUESTIONS

Sometimes people in your group may ask questions for which they just don't get a satisfactory answer. That's okay. In our journey with Jesus, sometimes He allows our minds to be unsatisfied so that our hearts can choose to trust Him more. God usually will reveal answers in time. If someone is struggling with an unanswered question, encourage him or her to talk to God about it and to trust in time He will clarify this issue. In the meanwhile, assure one another that "Wait" is one of God's answers to our prayers.

5

Walking As a Servant

CHAPTER OBJECTIVE: To follow Christ's example in giving ourselves as servants to others.

Since this is the last chapter in Book Three, devote extra time to reviewing this chapter's memory verse, as well as the previous four verses. Can you think of a new way to make Scripture memory review fun?

Provide your group with information on how to give financially to various missionaries and missionary organizations. You may also want to organize a service project to fill a need in your church or community.

> Good questions for discussion include 2, 5, 9, 14, and 16.

CHRIST YOUR EXAMPLE (Questions 1–4)

You might launch the discussion by asking a general question such as, "From this first section, what impressed you most about the servant heart of Jesus?"

You can tell by the puzzled faces in the group if one of your questions isn't understood. Restate the question in a different form.

Suggested for Discussion: Question 2
Why did Jesus become a servant?

Why do you think Jesus washed His disciples' feet (John 13:4-5)?

What images come to your mind when you think of a servant?

CHRIST'S DESIRE FOR YOU (Questions 5–7)

Suggested for Discussion: Question 5
Why did Jesus emphasize servanthood so much?

How do you feel after you have served someone voluntarily?

How do you feel when you are treated like a servant? How do you deal with these emotions?

Do you aspire to be great or to be a great servant?

GIVING YOURSELF (Questions 8–9)

Suggested for Discussion: Question 9
What do you think is the real test of being a servant?

How was Paul a servant for Jesus Christ?

KEYS TO BEING A SERVANT (Questions 10–18)

Suggested for Discussion: Questions 14 and 16

What is so important about humility?

How can you become a better servant this week?

CLOSING THE DISCUSSION

Consider various ways to close this discussion: Summary, Images and Quotes, Personal Applications, Going Deeper. Or simply ask, "From all we have studied, what can you give to others in order to truly serve them?"

PRAYER

Invite people to pray for one another, perhaps in pairs rather than as a whole group.

SCRIPTURE MEMORY REVIEW

Ask people how Scripture memory is helping them throughout the week. Take the time now (if you didn't at the beginning of your meeting) to review all five verses from Book Three.

REVIEW

This is the last chapter in Book Three. Perhaps it is time to review what has helped you most in your spiritual journey from everything you have studied in Book Three. Also discuss your plans to move on to Book Four. Ask members if there is anything you need to change to enrich your time together. Pass out copies of Book Four to those who will be continuing.

DISCUSSION TIP: DIGGING DEEPER

Some people always want more . . . maybe not every lesson but at various times. The Going Deeper section is designed to help people explore the Scriptures more and to consider their journeys with God at a deeper level. Encourage but don't demand people to go deeper. As you are closing the discussion, invite anyone who completed the Going Deeper section to share briefly.

THE CHARACTER OF A FOLLOWER OF JESUS

1

The Call to Fruitful Living

CHAPTER OBJECTIVE: To understand that living life to the fullest requires holiness in our thoughts, speech, and actions.

You may want to review the Wheel and Hand Illustrations as you begin Book Four. Ask the group members to consider how they desire God to mature them in the coming weeks and months. Then ask them to select one aspect of the Wheel Illustration and one aspect of the Hand Illustration that they desire to grow in. You might also invite them to write out specific ways in which they could deepen and develop in the two areas they select.

Also read together the introductions to Book Four called "Building for Quality" and "Why Focus on Character Now?"

Make a conscious effort to help each group member feel relaxed and part of the group.

> Good questions for discussion include 1, 2, 3, 8, 10, 15, 16, and 17.

GROWING IN THE FRUIT OF THE SPIRIT (Questions 1–6)

As you begin Book Four, you may find it helpful to review the material for leaders at the beginning of this book. This will remind you of important principles for discussion. For instance, you might launch the discussion by asking a general question such as, "From the first six questions, what impressed you most about growing in the fruit of the Spirit?"

By the time you have come this far in the *Design for Discipleship* series, you have had considerable experience in leading discussions. So you already know how important it is to listen closely to your group members' answers and choose one to ask a follow-up question. You are probably becoming more proficient at thinking of good follow-up questions on the spot. So the questions we provide here simply supplement this approach.

Suggested for Discussion: Questions 1, 2, and 3

How would you explain John 15:1-5 to someone else?

Why does God desire us to be fruitful?

What is the relationship between the teachings in John 15:1-5 and Galatians 5:22-23?

Which qualities listed in Matthew 5:3-12 do you feel the person on your right most exhibits in his or her life?

GROWING IN CHARACTER (Questions 7–13)

Suggested for Discussion: Questions 8 and 10

What changes do you want to see in your character?

Name someone you believe has godly wisdom. What do you observe in this person that you consider wise?

GROWING IN THE JOY OF HOLY LIVING (Questions 14–18)

Suggested for Discussion: Questions 15, 16, and 17

What would a life full of joy look like to you? Have you ever seen someone full of joy and yet weeping? Explain.

CLOSING THE DISCUSSION

People often remember most whatever is spoken last in a discussion. Use the last five to ten minutes of your discussion time to reinforce the central points of the lesson. You can do this by asking group members a summary application question such as Question 13-e, or a general question such as, "In which of these areas—thoughts, speech, or actions—do you feel God wants you to concentrate on most in developing more holiness?"

Other effective ways to close your discussion are to read the Points to Remember, to discuss an image or quote that especially touched someone, or to share something from the Going Deeper section (which is optional).

PRAYER

Don't neglect praying together. It is far more important to talk *with* God than it is to talk *about* God during the study. Enjoy worship and praise, as well as times of prayer requests.

SCRIPTURE MEMORY REVIEW

If your group has agreed to memorize and review Scripture together, be sure to reserve time for review. Review the verse for this week. This could be in pairs while people are gathering before your session or all together at the end.

DISCUSSION TIP: COLEADING A GROUP

If you don't already have a coleader to help you lead the group, consider asking someone from the group to do this or begin rotating leadership among several members. An effective leader is always looking to develop leadership in others.

2

Authentic Love in Action

CHAPTER OBJECTIVE: To see that love requires a deliberate decision of the will, an attitude of humility, and a desire to live this way.

For a project in character growth, suggest that each group member read and pray over a chapter of Proverbs each day for a month as a quiet-time exercise. Discuss together week by week the things you are learning from Proverbs.

> Good questions for discussion include 1, 2, 7, 8, 12, 13, and 18.

WHAT IS AUTHENTIC LOVE? (Questions 1–4)

You might launch discussion of this chapter by asking a general question such as, "From the first four questions, what is the best thing you observed about authentic love?"

You could also ask a group member to read the quote from Philip Yancey as a discussion starter.

Suggested for Discussion: Questions 1 and 2
 What do you think it means that "love never fails" (1 Corinthians 13:8)?

LOVING UNSELFISHLY (Questions 5–7)

Suggested for Discussion: Question 7
 What is the relationship between knowing about real love and showing it?

 Does God limit His love to anyone? Explain your answer.

 How has God's love been unselfish to you?

LOVE IN HUMILITY (Questions 8–12)

Suggested for Discussion: Questions 8 and 12
 Is there ever a proper time to have pride in your wisdom, strength, or riches (Jeremiah 9:23-24)? Explain.

 How do you feel about growing in humility? Do you desire humility? Do you seek humility?

LOVE IN SPEECH (Questions 13–15)

Suggested for Discussion: Question 13
 Why is speech so important in regard to love?

 How do you affirm others with words? What is generally their response?

LOVE IN GOOD WORKS (Questions 16–19)

Suggested for Discussion: Question 18 (Love Reality Check)
 What are some good works you can think of that you can do? And why would you do them?

CLOSING THE DISCUSSION

In closing this discussion, you may ask members to summarize the main points themselves, to read the Points to Remember, to comment on an Image or Quote, to share a personal Application, or to share from the Going Deeper section. Of course, don't try to do all of these, but select the ones that seem most appropriate for the flow of the discussion. A general summary application question for this session might be, "What deliberate decisions of the will should you make in order to show love to others in your life?"

Make an effort to meet with group members at least occasionally outside your regular discussion session. Use the time to help them individually in their spiritual growth and to discuss their concerns and questions.

PRAYER

Ask group members if they have any prayer requests, and pray over these as you close.

SCRIPTURE MEMORY REVIEW

If your group has agreed to memorize and review Scripture together, be sure to reserve time for review. Review the verses for this week and previous weeks.

DISCUSSION TIP: LISTEN MORE CLOSELY

Listening is a core skill in leading a discussion. Listen closely to the ideas people share. Listen more closely to the emotional responses of people. Ask "feeling" questions to unpack what you have heard.

CHAPTER

3

Purity of Life

CHAPTER OBJECTIVE: To recognize daily the importance of God's moral absolutes in our relationships with others, and to depend on the Scriptures as our authority for moral living.

> Good questions for discussion include 4, 6, 7, 9, 10, 13, 15, 17, and 23.

GOD'S STANDARD (Questions 1–5)

You might launch the discussion by reading the introduction to the chapter, or by reading the quote by Susanna Wesley. Then you could launch into the first section by asking a general question such as, "As you consider this first section, what did you discover about God's standard for the purity of our lives?"

Suggested for Discussion: Question 4
    How can we have a pure heart?

How can we meet God's standards realistically?

THE IMPORTANCE OF PERSONAL PURITY (Questions 6–10)

Suggested for Discussion: Questions 6, 7, 9, and 10

What effect does impurity have on your relationship with God?

Why is sexual immorality wrong?

THE PATH TO PURITY (Questions 11–18)

Suggested for Discussion: Questions 13, 15, and 17

Take the time to discuss the quote by Craig Gross and Mike Foster.

What are the first steps on the path to purity?

What does it mean to clothe ourselves with the Lord Jesus (Romans 13:14)?

PERSPECTIVE ON MARRIAGE (Questions 19–24)

Suggested for Discussion: Question 23

What does it mean in God's eyes for a man and a woman to be married?

Why do you think God uses marriage as a metaphor to describe the relationship between Christ and the church (Ephesians 5:21-33)?

How does this metaphor affect your thoughts and feelings about purity?

CLOSING THE DISCUSSION

Even though the Going Deeper section is optional in every chapter, your group may benefit from reading this together and then discussing ways we can avoid being trapped by sexual sin.

A good way to close each session is to summarize what has been discussed, motivate the group by sharing with them how important this topic is, and finally close in group prayer.

PRAYER

The topic of this chapter invites people to be authentic and vulnerable about some very personal, and perhaps painful, parts of their lives. It is good to reinforce the commitment made by group members to keep confidential all things shared in the group.

SCRIPTURE MEMORY REVIEW

If your group has agreed to memorize and review Scripture together, be sure to allow time for review. Review the verse for this week and previous weeks. Perhaps mention how Scripture memory helped you during the last week.

DISCUSSION TIP: BELIEVE GOD FOR CHANGE

True spiritual growth comes from the work of the Holy Spirit. Ask God to help you and each person in your group respond willingly to His ways of refining your character in the area of personal purity. And believe that God will change you.

4

Integrity in Living

CHAPTER OBJECTIVE: To practice honesty and trustworthiness in every area of life.

Suggest reading about the life of Joseph (Genesis 37–50) as an extra project. You can discuss this in your next session.

Remember that unless each member of your group has knowledge to share, the discussion method will not work. Encourage each member to complete his or her study preparation each week, and keep the discussion time centered on what the Scriptures say and how they can be applied to daily life.

> Good questions for discussion include 4, 7, 11, 14, 16, 17, and 18.

THE STRUGGLE FOR INTEGRITY (Questions 1–5)

As in the previous chapter, this topic invites you and your group members to explore some very personal aspects of character where many of us struggle. After having someone read the introduction, you might launch the discussion by asking a general question about your group members' struggle for integrity such as, "What stood out to you from this first section about our common human struggle for integrity?"

Suggested for Discussion: Question 4
Why do you think it is such a difficult battle to maintain our integrity?

Why are our hearts so deceptive — and so easily deceived?

What is your biggest struggle in maintaining integrity?

LACK OF INTEGRITY EXPOSED (Questions 6–11)

Suggested for Discussion: Questions 7 and 11
What is our conscience?

What emotions are pricked by our conscience?

Why do you think Jesus was so critical of hypocrisy?

How do you respond to others' hypocrisy? To your own hypocrisy?

THE PRACTICE OF HONESTY (Questions 12–14)

Suggested for Discussion: Question 14
Is there ever a time when a believer should not submit to an authority? If so, when?

HONESTY IN SPEECH (Questions 15–21)

Suggested for Discussion: Questions 16, 17, and 18
Why does speech begin in the heart?

How does what you say reveal who you are?

CLOSING THE DISCUSSION

Select from the several ways you might bring this discussion to a close. You might ask, "In closing, why do you believe you should demonstrate honesty in every area of your life?" Or you could ask a few members to share personal applications by saying, "As you reflect back over your study of Scripture, how have these passages impacted you this week? How can you apply these to your daily life this coming week?"

Or, if it has been some time since you invited your group members to process images, you might want to try that instead.

PRAYER

Don't forget to share answers to prayer and reasons to praise God as well as requests. This topic also lends itself to a time of personal confession. Scripture encourages us to confess our sins to one another as well as to God because this brings us out of hiddenness into the light. If someone in your group needs to make restitution or take some other step to walk in integrity, help him or her do that as well.

SCRIPTURE MEMORY REVIEW

If your group has agreed to memorize and review Scripture together, be sure to reserve time for review — either at the end of the session or at the beginning. If you have time, ask group members to share how Scripture memory is helping them throughout the week. Since there is only one more chapter left in Book Four, take time to review all four verses memorized so far, and come prepared to quote all five verses from this book at the next session.

DISCUSSION TIP: CONSIDER STARTING A NEW GROUP

Maybe it's time to start a new group. Here's a suggestion. Ask two people in your group to prayerfully consider starting a new group. Ask if they have friends or friends of friends they can invite. You can be a sounding board to them as they encounter questions.

5

Character Development in Suffering

CHAPTER OBJECTIVE: To know that God allows suffering in our lives to help produce godly character in us, and to be thankful in all circumstances.

Since this is the last chapter in Book Four, take extra time at the beginning of your session to review your five memory verses and to motivate your members to persist in this valuable discipline of hiding God's Word in their hearts.

As you discuss this topic, try to differentiate between suffering for Christ's sake, suffering because we live in a fallen world with other sinful people, and suffering as a consequence of our own mistakes and wrongdoing.

> Good questions for discussion include 2, 3, 4, 9, 11, 19, 20, and 21.

GOD'S ULTIMATE CONTROL (Questions 1–4)

As you launch the discussion of this topic, remember that the skillful use of questions is a crucial factor in the success of a group discussion. Plan your questions carefully. For instance, after having someone read the chapter introduction, you might launch the discussion by asking a general question such as, "From these first four questions, what impressed you most about the reality that God is ultimately in control?"

Suggested for Discussion: Questions 2, 3, and 4

What does Genesis 50:20 reveal about Joseph's character?

What does it mean to you that in all things God works for our good?

THE PURPOSE OF SUFFERING (Questions 5–9)

Suggested for Discussion: Question 9

Why must followers of Jesus suffer?

What are some of the kinds of suffering we may have to endure?

YOUR RESPONSE TO SUFFERING (Questions 10–18)

Suggested for Discussion: Question 11

Why are our attitudes in life so important?

When suffering, is it ever right to ask God, "Why me?" Explain your answer.

GROWING THROUGH SUFFERING (Questions 19–22)

Suggested for Discussion: Questions 19, 20, and 21

Why does hope follow suffering, perseverance, and character?

When does God discipline us?

How does God comfort us?

How have you experienced suffering? How has this affected your relationship with God?

CLOSING THE DISCUSSION

Consider closing your discussion by doing Option A from the Going Deeper section together. You could also include either a Summary, more time of sharing personal Applications, or processing an Image or Quote from the chapter. If any of your group members have experienced or are currently experiencing deep suffering, be prepared to come alongside them with sympathy and prayer support.

SCRIPTURE MEMORY REVIEW

If your group has agreed to memorize and review Scripture together, be sure to reserve time for reviewing all five verses from this book. Encourage them to go back and review verses memorized from previous books as well. The key to retaining memorized verses is Review, Review, Review!

REVIEW AND PRAYER

Since this is the last chapter in Book Four, devote a few minutes to reviewing your time together over the last weeks. Encourage members to continue in their series by studying Book Five. You might ask questions such as:

"How did you like Book Four?"

"What was the most helpful thing from our study together over these weeks?"

"Would you like to go on to Book Five?"

"Is there anything we need to change in order to enrich our time together?"

Then hand out Book Five to those who will continue, and agree on the next assignment and meeting arrangements. Close in prayer.

DISCUSSION TIP: CHANGING LOCATIONS

Over time, groups tend to get into ruts. Sometimes changing locations will help you approach your discussion differently. These changes can positively impact your growing deeper as a group. You might shift to a different member's home or even meet at a coffeehouse.

FOUNDATIONS FOR FAITH

CHAPTER

1

Who Is God?

CHAPTER OBJECTIVE: To respond deeply to our awesome God, especially in praise and worship.

As your group begins Book Five, it may be good to reflect on how God has been deepening your relationships with Him and with each other over the months. Then get into Book Five by reading the introduction called "Getting God's Perspective."

Don't give the impression that as the leader you do not need help in the areas you are discussing. Use the word *we* rather than *you*. Say, "How should *we* apply this passage?"

> Good questions for discussion include 1, 2, 5, 6, 12, 14, and 17.

WHAT IS GOD LIKE? (Questions 1–8)

You might launch the discussion by having someone read the chapter introduction or the quote by S. J. Hill (following question 2). Then ask a general question such as, "As you consider this first section, did something in particular stand out to you about what God is like?"

Just as in previous leading experiences, you should listen closely to your group members' answers and choose one to ask a follow-up question.

Suggested for Discussion: Questions 1, 2, 5, and 6
Who does God say He is?

How does it make you feel to know that God is jealous *for* you (not jealous *of* you)?

Which of God's attributes do you think you know the least about?

WHAT DOES GOD DO? (Questions 11–12)

Suggested for Discussion: Question 12
How does God demonstrate His power?

How is God's love expressed in action?

WHAT DOES GOD EXPECT FROM YOU? (Questions 13–17)

Suggested for Discussion: Questions 14 and 17
Why does God desire anything from us?

How does one experience a broken spirit and a contrite heart?

Why is it so important to worship God?

CLOSING THE DISCUSSION

By now you know that there are several ways to bring a discussion to a close. Use the last five to ten minutes of your time together to invite sharing about personal Applications, to comment on a Quote or Image from the chapter, or to share a highlight from the optional Going Deeper section.

You will also notice that in Book Five no summary statements are provided for you. Your group members can glance over each section and summarize the main points of each in a sentence or two.

PRAYER

This topic lends itself to worship and praise in prayer, as well as praying for each other's needs and requests. Let the Prayer Pause (following question 5) lead you into prayer.

SCRIPTURE MEMORY REVIEW

If your group has agreed to memorize and review Scripture together, be sure to reserve time to review the memory verse for this week. Some groups prefer to review memory verses in pairs at the beginning of the meeting while others are arriving. Other groups review verses together at the end. Consider reviewing out loud, in writing, in unison, or in other ways.

DISCUSSION TIP: INTIMACY WITH GOD

The primary goal of Bible study is to grow in a deep, intimate relationship with God and to authentically worship Him for who He is—the Sovereign Triune God who jealously loves us. As you lead your discussion group, continue to remind those in your group that this is the goal.

CHAPTER

2

The Authority of God's Word

CHAPTER OBJECTIVE: To gain greater life dependence on the Scriptures as the trustworthy Word of God.

Reading either the introduction to the chapter or the quote from John Stott (following question 4) would be a good way to begin discussion of this topic.

> Good questions for discussion include 2, 4, 5, 14, 16, 22, and 23.

GOD'S REVELATION THROUGH THE SCRIPTURES
(Questions 1–4)

Prepare your own launching questions for this section. Or ask something such as "As you consider this first section, what did you observe about God's revelation to us through the Scriptures?"

After a section has been discussed, summarize the direction your discussion has taken. This reinforces what you have been talking about. Then summarize the entire discussion at the end of your time together.

Suggested for Discussion: Questions 2 and 4
On what basis does the Bible's authority rest?

What difference does it make who wrote the Scriptures?

What does it mean that God's Word is "living and active"?

JESUS' CONFIDENCE IN THE SCRIPTURES (Questions 5–10)

Suggested for Discussion: Question 5
What can we learn from Jesus' encounter with Satan?

OUR CONFIDENCE IN THE SCRIPTURES (Questions 11–15)

Suggested for Discussion: Question 14
How confident are you in the Scriptures?

How can we know the Scriptures are reliable?

OUR SOURCE OF LIFE (Questions 16–23)

Suggested for Discussion: Questions 16, 22, and 23
How can the Bible be sufficient for every area of life?

Are you committed to following God and obeying His Word? Explain.

What is the most important way the Bible makes a difference in your life today?

CLOSING THE DISCUSSION

Select one or more of the following ways to close your discussion: Going Deeper, Application, Images and Quotes, or a summary by one of the members.

PRAYER

For a change, perhaps invite members to share their requests in pairs and pray for one another in twos rather than as a large group.

SCRIPTURE MEMORY REVIEW

If your group has agreed to memorize and review Scripture together, they may be lagging in motivation or discipline. But don't chastise or shame people for struggling. Recognize that Satan opposes this valuable spiritual exercise. Seek to motivate your members to continue diligently.

DISCUSSION TIP: A GRAND VIEW OF REALITY

As we study Scripture we are gaining a grand view of reality. When discussing your studies, consider periodically asking people to share how the study has impacted their view of reality.

3

The Holy Spirit

CHAPTER OBJECTIVE: To accept how the Holy Spirit is present and active in each believer and gives gifts to each one.

Emphasize to your group that the way of discipleship is not easy. Rather, it is costly. Help them see the cost. Also reassure them that the Holy Spirit is always available and indwelling to empower them to live as disciples of Christ.

Have someone read aloud the information about the Trinity on page 42.

> Good questions for discussion include 1, 4, 7, 9, 15, and 21.

WHO IS THE HOLY SPIRIT? (Questions 1–3)

Prepare your own launching questions for each section of this study. Then listen and follow up with probing questions inviting others to process their observations and ideas a bit more.

Suggested for Discussion: Question 1

How would you describe the Holy Spirit?

How would you explain the Trinity?

WHO HAS THE HOLY SPIRIT? (Questions 4–8)

Suggested for Discussion: Questions 4 and 7

How does a person acquire the Holy Spirit?

What does it mean that you are a temple of God?

THE WORK OF THE HOLY SPIRIT (Questions 9–12)

Suggested for Discussion: Question 9

What does the Holy Spirit do for believers?

How does the Holy Spirit help you walk with God?

THE GIFTS OF THE HOLY SPIRIT (Questions 13–16)

Suggested for Discussion: Question 15

What are the spiritual gifts you believe you have?

How can you serve others with these gifts?

How can you affirm the gifts of others?

YOUR RESPONSIBILITY (Questions 17–21)

Suggested for Discussion: Question 21

What does it mean to "grieve the Holy Spirit" (Ephesians 4:30)?

How can we bring joy to the Holy Spirit?

CLOSING THE DISCUSSION

People often remember most whatever is spoken last in a discussion. Use the last five to ten minutes to reinforce the central points of this lesson. You can do this by asking group members to summarize each section in a sentence or two, or to comment on an Image or Quote they liked, or to share something from the optional Going Deeper section.

PRAYER

Invite people to pray over needs and requests. But also encourage them to share issues of their hearts, motives, and emotions. If you do the same, they will feel safe to follow.

SCRIPTURE MEMORY REVIEW

If you didn't review verses at the beginning of the meeting, do so now.

DISCUSSION TIP: ISSUES OF THE HEART

The living Word of God exposes the deep issues of our hearts. As a discussion leader you can encourage people to examine their motives and emotions in light of the Scripture. One way to encourage others in sharing is by sharing your heart with them.

4

Spiritual Warfare

CHAPTER OBJECTIVE: To realize that every follower of Jesus is engaged in a spiritual battle with Satan, and to receive the means for victory that God has given us.

Reading the introduction to the chapter would be a good way to get into this chapter.

> Good questions for discussion include 1, 3, 5, 6, 8, 10, 13, 15, 17, and 19.

TWO KINGDOMS (Questions 1–3)

Prepare a good launching question for this section. For instance, you could ask, "What stood out to you from the first three questions about the two kingdoms?"

In asking questions your goal is not merely to get answers, but to bring about discussion. Avoid questions that require only short, categorical answers.

Suggested for Discussion: Questions 1 and 3
What does it mean to you that Satan has a kingdom?

OUR BATTLE (Questions 4–5)

Suggested for Discussion: Question 5
What battle are we in?

What does Satan desire for you?

KNOW YOUR ENEMY (Questions 6–10)

Suggested for Discussion: Questions 6, 8, and 10
How do you know you have a spiritual enemy?

How does Satan try to deceive you?

How should you respond practically to Satan (1 Peter 5:8-9)?

THE CONFLICT WITH SIN (Questions 11–15)

Suggested for Discussion: Questions 13 and 15
Why do we have such a battle with sin?

What does the world system have to offer?

What is the "crown of life" that God promises to those who love Him (James 1:12)?

THE ASSURANCE OF VICTORY (Questions 16–17)

Suggested for Discussion: Question 17
What is the extent of Satan's power?

Why was Christ's death so essential for us?

What is the victory God gives us?

DAILY VICTORY (Questions 18–22)

Suggested for Discussion: Question 19

What to you are the most important factors for living in day-by-day obedience to the Lord?

How are you doing in gaining daily victory?

CLOSING THE DISCUSSION

Select from the several ways of bringing a discussion to a close: Summary, Images and Quotes, Going Deeper, or Application. Or you might ask the group to respond to a summary application question such as, "What weapons are you now using most as you wage spiritual warfare?"

PRAYER

Invite members to pray over specific areas where they are experiencing spiritual warfare or attack from Satan. You may need to do intercessory prayer for some. Pray in the confidence that Jesus has already won the victory over Satan.

SCRIPTURE MEMORY REVIEW

In pairs, take the time to review all four memory verses from Book Five this week. Challenge members to write out their verses during the week to check for accuracy.

5

The Return of Christ

CHAPTER OBJECTIVE: To grow in our expectant hope for the return of Christ.

Since this is the last chapter in Book Five, you may need to devote extra time to Scripture memory, if that is part of your group's commitment.

Start the discussion by reading the introduction to the chapter.

> Good questions for discussion include 1, 3, 6, 7, 8, 16, 18, and 21.

THE PROMISE OF HIS RETURN (Questions 1–4)

Prepare your own launching question for this section. Also remember that a competent leader always respects the thoughts, opinions, and feelings of the members of his or her group, thus creating a positive atmosphere for discussion.

Suggested for Discussion: Questions 1 and 3

How do you know Jesus Christ will return?

What do you think it means that Christ is preparing a place for us?

What does it mean to you that Jesus will come in glory (Matthew 16:27; Mark 13:26-27)?

CONDITIONS PRECEDING HIS RETURN (Questions 5–7)

Suggested for Discussion: Questions 6 and 7

How would you summarize what the world will be like just before Jesus comes?

How do present events indicate that prophecy is being fulfilled?

EVENTS AT HIS RETURN (Questions 8–14)

Suggested for Discussion: Question 8

Describe in your own words the future events surrounding Jesus' return.

How does your knowledge of these events affect your life now?

WHAT HIS RETURN MEANS TO YOU (Questions 15–21)

Suggested for Discussion: Questions 16, 18, and 21

What aspect of His coming do you most look forward to?

CLOSING THE DISCUSSION

Select one creative way to close this session. For instance, you might ask, "From everything that we have learned, what are you motivated to do by knowing Christ is coming again?"

SCRIPTURE MEMORY REVIEW

Since this is the last week in Book Five, take a few extra minutes to review all five memory verses. If members have fallen behind, encourage them to catch up before Book Six. Also invite someone to share how a memorized verse has helped him or her personally or in witnessing or teaching others.

REVIEW AND PRAYER

This is the last chapter in Book Five. Perhaps it is time to review what has helped you most in your spiritual journey from everything you have studied in Book Five. Also discuss your plans to move on to Book Six. Ask members if there is anything you need to change to enrich your time together. Pass out copies of Book Six to those who will be continuing. Close in prayer.

DISCUSSION TIP: CARE FOR NATURE

God's first commands to Adam and Eve included the mandate to care for nature. This mandate can be overlooked in our modern societies. Ask your group to consider how they might return to this initial command.

GROWING IN
DISCIPLESHIP

1

What Is a Disciple?

CHAPTER OBJECTIVE: To make progress in the commitments required of a disciple of Jesus Christ.

As you begin your study together in Book Six, remember that God blesses you so that you can be a blessing to others. The Great Commission means that you are not only invited to be His disciple but also to participate with Him in making disciples! At the heart of Book Six is the theme of passing on the blessings of Christ to others. To help your group members engage with this theme, you might begin by reading together the introduction to Book Six called "Yours to Give."

> Good questions for discussion include 1, 2, 6, 8, 11, 14, 16, and 21.

JESUS' INVITATION TO A SPECIAL RELATIONSHIP
(Questions 1–5)

By this time, you as a leader have developed skills in inviting people to discuss the fruits of their personal Bible study. What general launching question might you ask to start off in this section? Write it here:

You have also had ample experience listening closely to how your group members respond and asking follow-up questions that take the discussion a bit deeper. Take a few minutes to refresh your memory of these skills by rereading the material at the beginning of this book. As you do, what two or three suggestions stand out to you that you would like to practice during Book Six? Write them here:

As you lead through Book Six, keep in mind that two broad goals for disciples of Jesus Christ are sharing their faith and helping other followers of Jesus grow as disciples. Evaluate how your group members are doing in these areas and help them where you can.

Suggested for Discussion: Questions 1 and 2
How would you describe a disciple of Jesus?

How can you tell if you love anyone or anything else above Jesus?

THE DISCIPLE IS A LEARNER (Questions 6–10)
Suggested for Discussion: Questions 6 and 8
From whom do you feel you learn the most?

What are some things you do not like to receive instruction or correction for?

How do you ensure that you are learning from the heart as well as from the head?

THE COST OF DISCIPLESHIP (Questions 11–14)

Suggested for Discussion: Questions 11 and 14

Why does Christ want us to count the cost of our discipleship?

Why is there a cost?

What could it cost you *not* to be Jesus' disciple?

DILIGENCE AND DISCIPLINE (Questions 15–23)

Suggested for Discussion: Questions 16 and 21

How can we keep our eyes on Jesus?

What do you think it means to walk consistently with Christ?

On a scale from 1-10 (10 is extremely consistent), how consistent are you in your walk with Christ?

How does focusing on consistency in spiritual disciplines affect your heart connection with God?

How can an undisciplined person become more disciplined?

CLOSING THE DISCUSSION

Now that you have had experience leading a small group through Bible study discussion, you are hopefully developing a sense of timing. You know that it isn't essential to discuss every question. Rather it is valuable to invite members to share the most important insights they have gained and the applications God has impressed on them from their personal study.

You also have learned that bringing the discussion to a close — and doing it on time — is an art to be developed. Throughout this study we have tried to provide several creative ways to do this. Which of the following methods will you use in this chapter to close the discussion: Summary, Going Deeper, additional Applications, or commenting on Images and Quotes? Is there another method the Lord has impressed on you — perhaps an appropriate song, personal illustration, visual aid, or a general summary question such as, "What do you think are your most important commitments as a disciple of Jesus Christ?" Be creative in how you close each discussion.

SCRIPTURE MEMORY REVIEW

If your group has agreed to memorize and review Scripture together, include in your plan when and how you will review each week's verse. If you have been reviewing memory verses at the end, try shifting that to the beginning. The material at the beginning of Book Two in this Leader's Guide provides several creative suggestions and motivational verses on Scripture memory. Review that material now and write below two or three ways you will bring creativity and variety to your group's Scripture memory and review during Book Six.

PRAYER

Close your time together in prayer. Encourage people (by your example) to pray briefly over whatever personal applications God has impressed on their hearts about the topic studied. We need God's help in whatever He calls us to do.

DISCUSSION TIP: SERVING OUTSIDE THE GROUP

Bible study is not meant to be an end in itself. And groups can become ingrown. In order to help your group grow in their walk with God, discuss how you can serve others. Brainstorm some options you have to serve others as a group. Then select one of these options and plan to put it into action. Serving others together will knit your members together in ways that discussion alone cannot do.

2

The Responsible Steward

CHAPTER OBJECTIVE: To grow in our responsibility to God for the way we use what He has given us.

The concept of a "steward" may be a bit obscure for people today. To help your group understand this theme, read the introduction to the chapter. Perhaps open the discussion by asking, "How would you describe the tasks and character of a modern-day trustee? How is this similar to — and different from — the 'steward' in the Bible?"

> Good questions for discussion include 3, 4, 7, 8, 12, 14, and 18.

STEWARDS OF GOD'S RESOURCES (Questions 1–3)

Write here (or in the margin of your study guide) a launching question that you might use to open the discussion of the first section.

As a leader, if you allow the discussion to wander aimlessly, it will soon become boring. Reestablish the purpose and direction of the discussion when you need to.

Suggested for Discussion: Question 3
Can you think of areas in which you should be a faithful steward?

USE OF TIME (Questions 4–9)

Suggested for Discussion: Questions 4, 7, and 8
What are some guidelines for how a disciple should use his or her time?

Why is work essential?

What are your priorities for using your limited time?

USE OF GIFTS (Questions 10–12)

Suggested for Discussion: Question 12
What do you believe are your spiritual gifts?

How can you develop these gifts?

How can you serve others with your gifts?

CARE OF THE BODY (Questions 13–16)

Suggested for Discussion: Question 14
How can you honor God with your body?

USE OF MONEY (Questions 17–22)

Suggested for Discussion: Question 18

> What to you are the most important scriptural principles regarding the use of our money?

> How can we serve God and *not* money? How can we serve God *with* our money?

> How does your heart respond to the idea of giving money in the name of Jesus?

> Do you have a plan for giving? Explain.

CLOSING THE DISCUSSION

As you draw your discussion to a close, select one or more of these methods: sharing a personal Application, commenting on an Image or Quote, summarizing key principles. In what area do you think you most need to exercise better stewardship?

PRAYER

No doubt this topic has prompted your members to identify specific ways they can be better stewards of their resources. Take the time to pray over these, perhaps in pairs rather than in the whole group.

SCRIPTURE MEMORY REVIEW

Plan to review your memory verses together — either at the beginning or the end. Which creative ways to review might you use this week to keep Scripture memory motivating for your group?

DISCUSSION TIP: SAFE SHARING ENVIRONMENTS

From the first time your group meets, building a safe sharing environment is essential. Remind your group that what is shared during the group discussion stays within the group. Also let them know that a discussion is about process—every answer doesn't have to be the best or even right. It is important that we process our spiritual journeys with others within safe environments.

3

Helping Others
Find Christ

CHAPTER OBJECTIVE: To make progress in leading others toward Christ.

Discuss the idea of having at least some of the group members begin an evangelistic Bible study group in their home with their nonbelieving friends. Help them plan and begin this. Challenge your group in this and other ways of sharing the gospel.

> Good questions for discussion include 1, 7, 8, 9, 13, 14, 18, and 22.

PARTNERING WITH GOD (Questions 1–6)

During the discussion, work at combining the contributions of individual group members to show that together you can find needed answers and solve common problems.

What launching question will you use to open the discussion of the questions? Write it here:

Suggested for Discussion: Question 1

Why do you think God would extend an invitation for us to partner with Him?

How does your heart respond to that invitation?

OVERCOMING OBSTACLES (Questions 7–10)

Suggested for Discussion: Questions 7, 8, and 9

What fears do you have as you share Christ with others?

What other follow-up questions can you think of? Write them here:

LIVING AS AN INSIDER (Questions 11–16)

Suggested for Discussion: Questions 13 and 14

How can we live as followers of Jesus in the midst of people who don't follow Him?

CONVERSING THE GOSPEL (Questions 17–20)

Suggested for Discussion: Question 18

What are your favorite passages pertaining to the gospel?

What have been your experiences in discussing Jesus with others?

PARTICIPATING IN A NEW BIRTH (Questions 21–23)

Suggested for Discussion: Question 22

How might you use one of the verses given in encouraging a person to accept Christ?

What other follow-up questions can you think of for this section? Write them here:

CLOSING THE DISCUSSION

As you bring this discussion to a close, consider inviting members to finish this sentence: "My greatest difficulty in leading others toward Christ is . . ." Or use another method, such as Summary, Image and Quotes, or playing a motivating song related to sharing Christ.

PRAYER

In your prayer time, invite members to pray specifically for their seeking friends and family members whom they would like to "converse the gospel" with in the coming weeks.

SCRIPTURE MEMORY REVIEW

Which method of Scripture memory review do you plan to use this week? Write it here:

DISCUSSION TIP: JOURNAL REVIEWS

Each week people have been journaling. Once in a while ask people to review their journals over the past several weeks. Are there any trends they are seeing in their spiritual growth?

4

Establishing

CHAPTER OBJECTIVE: To move toward loving and practically helping a young follower of Jesus grow into spiritual maturity.

Read the introduction to this chapter to get the discussion started. Perhaps invite members to reminisce about their own first few months or years as young believers. What kind of help did they receive being established in their faith — if any?

> Good questions for discussion include 1, 5, 6, 11, 13, and 19.

WHAT IS ESTABLISHING? (Question 1)

The price of excellence is careful planning. Take the time you need to prepare adequately for each discussion session. This preparation includes prayer.

Write a simple launching question that you will use to open the discussion of the first section:

Suggested for Discussion: Question 1

What are the most important things you have to share with younger followers of Jesus?

In the space below, write additional follow-up questions that you might use for each section.

WHY ESTABLISHING? (Questions 2–5)

Suggested for Discussion: Question 5

What have been the major needs in your own life for growing spiritually?

THE WORTH OF EACH INDIVIDUAL (Questions 6–11)

Suggested for Discussion: Questions 6 and 11

As you consider your worth and the worth of others, how does your heart connect with the truths of this section?

How does this topic relate to helping younger followers of Jesus grow?

HELPING OTHERS GROW (Questions 12–16)

Suggested for Discussion: Question 13

Why is prayer important in helping someone else grow spiritually?

BEING AN EXAMPLE (Questions 17–21)

Suggested for Discussion: Question 19; Also read the quote by Eric Sandras (following question 21) and discuss.

Who in your life has provided the best example to help you grow spiritually?

Who is watching your life and considering your example?

CLOSING THE DISCUSSION

Several application questions are already in this study, so you may want to consider other ways to close the discussion, such as a Summary, commenting on an Image or Quote, or sharing from the Going Deeper section.

PRAYER

This is a great time to pray for young and growing followers of Christ who may be looking to you and your group members as examples. Pray for them as you close your discussion.

SCRIPTURE MEMORY REVIEW

With only one chapter left in Book Six, you will need to devote a few extra minutes to reviewing the memory verses. Encourage your members to review all five verses during the coming week.

DISCUSSION TIP: ASKING FOR COMMITMENT

People need to voice their commitments to others. Every once in a while, ask people what progress and commitments they have made in their walks with God.

5

World Vision

CHAPTER OBJECTIVE: To try to see the world from God's point of view.

This chapter will lift your sights beyond your own life and growth to glimpse what God is doing around the world. Consider posting a large world map to help visualize this global perspective.

Look together at the world map and breakdown of world religions on page 84. Discuss as a group the implications of what you see.

> Good questions for discussion include 1, 2, 9, and 12.

GOD'S CONCERN FOR THE WORLD (Questions 1–3)

If you are talking as much as half the time during your group discussion, you're talking too much. Don't give the group the idea that you are the source of truth. Truth should be discovered in and shared from the Scriptures. Help all your group members experience this.

You could ask someone in your group to read the quote by Dawson Trotman to get the discussion started. Then use a launching question with follow-up questions to discuss this section.

Suggested for Discussion: Questions 1 and 2
 What things have already developed your world vision?

THE WORLD TODAY (Questions 4–6)

Suggested for Discussion: "Look at the Fields" on page 85.
 Why do you think there are so few workers for the harvest?

SPIRITUAL GENERATIONS (Questions 7–9)

Suggested for Discussion: Question 9
 How would you explain the principle of spiritual generations?

HOW DO YOU FIT IN? (Questions 10–13)

Suggested for Discussion: Question 12
 What important things can we pray for that will reflect world vision?

 Are you investing your life, time, and money with the world in mind? What can you do to become more involved in reaching the world with the good news of Jesus Christ?

CLOSING THE DISCUSSION

One idea for closing this discussion about world vision is to process the Going Deeper section together, asking people how they are investing in the Great Commission in some tangible way. Or you could ask, "Do you feel you are better able now to see the world from God's point of view? Why or why not?"

SCRIPTURE MEMORY REVIEW

Take time now (or at the beginning) to review all five verses from Book Six together.

REVIEW AND PRAYER

This is the last chapter in Book Six. Perhaps it is time to review what has helped you most in your spiritual journey from everything you have studied in Book Six. Also explain to your group that Book Seven will involve learning an entirely new method of Bible study: the Book Analysis of 1 Thessalonians. Discuss your plans to move on to Book Seven. Ask members if there is anything you need to change to enrich your time together. Pass out copies of Book Seven to those who will be continuing. Also take the time to actually look at the first chapter and talk through the new method of study. Then close in prayer.

DISCUSSION TIP: MERCY AND ACCOUNTABILITY

We need people to hold us accountable to our commitments. And we need people to show mercy when we fail to live up to our commitments. As you lead your group you will have opportunity to show both over time. At an appropriate time, you may wish to discuss mutual accountability and mercy within your group

OUR HOPE IN CHRIST

Book Seven
Introduction

OVERALL OBJECTIVE: To grow toward Christlikeness and experience God in life and ministry by studying 1 Thessalonians. While we provide guidance through processes, methods, and study skills, our hope is that God will positively change lives.

1 Thessalonians: Your Survey

OBJECTIVE: To learn how to do a book survey by getting an overall view of 1 Thessalonians.

As you begin Book Seven, many of your group members — and perhaps you as well — are starting chapter analysis Bible study for the first time. This study method is not complex, and it will provide a wealth of enlightenment as you learn to see books of the Bible as a whole.

More so than in the first six books of *Design for Discipleship,* each person's written work will probably vary a good deal from anyone else's in the group. It is important to allow enough discussion time for each one to share his or her discoveries.

Encourage group members to take notes in their own books about what others are sharing. You should devote the largest portion of your time to a discussion of your overviews.

Personal concern and consideration are the keys to having a loving attitude toward your group members. How much do you care about their spiritual growth? How much do you respect their thoughts and feelings?

2-6

1 Thessalonians: Chapters 1–5

OBJECTIVE: To learn how to do chapter analysis in the Bible by carefully studying each chapter of 1 Thessalonians.

In your survey you looked at all of 1 Thessalonians. Now you are ready to look at its separate parts — chapter by chapter — to gain an even better understanding of this portion of Scripture. (Later you will look again at the book as a whole.)

Try to plan your time each week to have adequate discussion on every part of the study. The most important areas for discussion, however, will probably be your questions, conclusion, and applications, so allow plenty of time for these areas. One simple way to do this is for you to share conclusions you have come to or a personal application God impressed on you occasionally while going through the chapter — not just at the end.

For example, you might say something like this:

"One conclusion I came to about verses 2-4 is . . ."

"When I consider the principle in verse 4, I think God is moving me to apply it by . . ."

Again, remember that the conclusions and answers discovered by the group in their individual preparation may vary greatly. So make sure everyone contributes to the discussion.

Be sensitive to the new study skills members are being asked to develop. For example, some members will find Observations easy, but Cross-References difficult. If some group members are having difficulty in a particular area, have the others share how they are achieving success. Concentrate on this especially in the early chapters so the difficulties can be overcome as you progress through 1 Thessalonians.

In your discussion, do the group members display initiative and creative thinking? Encourage them to do this. Sometimes it is good to have a group member repeat and rephrase his or her ideas so they can be understood more clearly.

Remind the group that becoming an effective disciple of Jesus Christ is a process. Intimacy with God grows over time. Maturity in Christ involves steady, patient obedience to the things we know are right.

7

1 Thessalonians:
Your Summary

OBJECTIVE: To summarize your study of 1 Thessalonians, thus learning how to organize the results of a chapter analysis Bible study into practical, meaningful conclusions.

This could be your most enjoyable discussion time since you began *Design for Discipleship* — a good way to end this series.

Don't be surprised if your group still has many unanswered questions as you conclude your study of 1 Thessalonians. Remind them of the Bible's richness and how they will want to return again to study 1 Thessalonians and make new discoveries.

You may now want to plan together as a group to do a chapter analysis study of another book, such as Philippians or 1 John.

To help the group maintain motivation for doing personal Bible study on their own, have each member give reasons why Bible study is important to him or her.

As you go forward, consider starting new groups. Ask your group members to pair up and start groups of their own.

The essential Bible study series for twenty-first-century followers of Christ.

DFD 1
Your Life in Christ
ISBN 978-1-60006-004-5

This concise, easy-to-follow Bible study reveals what it means to accept God's love for you, keep Christ at the center of your life, and live in the power of the Spirit.

DFD 2
The Spirit-Filled Follower of Jesus
ISBN 978-1-60006-005-2

Learn what it means to be filled by the Spirit so that obedience, Bible study, prayer, fellowship, and witnessing become natural, meaningful aspects of your life.

DFD 3
Walking with Christ
ISBN 978-1-60006-006-9

Learn five vital aspects to living as a strong and mature disciple of Christ through this easy-to-understand Bible study.

DFD 4
The Character of a Follower of Jesus
ISBN 978-1-60006-007-6

This insightful, easy-to-grasp Bible study helps you understand and put into action the internal qualities and values that should drive your life as a disciple of Christ.

DFD 5
Foundations for Faith
ISBN 978-1-60006-008-3

This compelling Bible study will help you get a disciple's perspective on God, His Word, the Holy Spirit, spiritual warfare, and Christ's return.

DFD 6
Growing in Discipleship
ISBN 978-1-60006-009-0

This study will provide insight and encouragement to help you grow as a true disciple of Christ by learning to share the blessings you've received from God.

DFD 7
Our Hope in Christ
ISBN 978-1-60006-010-6

In this study of 1 Thessalonians, discover how to undertake a comprehensive analysis of a book of the Bible and gain effective Bible study principles that will last a lifetime.

NAVPRESS⬤

SUPPORT THE MINISTRY OF THE NAVIGATORS

The Navigators' calling is to advance the Gospel of Jesus and His Kingdom into the nations through spiritual generations of laborers living and discipling among the lost.

Navigators have invested their lives in people for more than 75 years, coming alongside them life-on-life to help them passionately know Christ and to make Him known.

The U.S. Navigators' ministry touches lives in varied settings, including college campuses, military bases, downtown offices, urban neighborhoods, prisons, and youth camps.

Dedicated to helping people navigate spiritually, The Navigators aim to make a permanent difference in the lives of people around the world. The Navigators help their communities of friends to follow Christ passionately and equip them effectively to go out and do the same.

To learn more about donating to The Navigators' ministry, go to **www.navigators.org/us/support** or call toll-free at **1-866-568-7827**.